The Baskervilles:

A Comic Thriller Starring Shirley Holmes and Jennie Watson

Adapted and dramatized

by

KENT R. BROWN

Inspired by the novel by

SIR ARTHUR CONAN DOYLE

Dramatic Publishing

Woodstock, Illinois • England • Australia • New Zealand

*** NOTICE ***

IMPORTANT BILLING AND CREDIT REQUIREMENTS

All producers of the play *must* give credit to the author of the play in all programs distributed in connection with performances of the play and in all instances in which the title of the play appears for purposes of advertising, publicizing or otherwise exploiting the play and/or a production. The name of the author *must* also appear on a separate line, on which no other name appears, immediately following the title, and *must* appear in size of type not less than fifty percent (50%) the size of the title type. Biographical information on the author, if included in the playbook, may be used in all programs. *In all programs this notice must appear:*

"Produced by special arrangement with
THE DRAMATIC PUBLISHING COMPANY of Woodstock, Illinois"

The Hound of the Baskervilles:
A Comic Thriller Starring Shirley Holmes and Jennie Watson

A Play in Two Acts
for 6 men, 7 women, plus 11-40 either gender

CHARACTERS:

JENNIE WATSON: The niece of John Watson. Studying medicine. Methodical, loyal, courageous.

SHIRLEY HOLMES: The niece of Sherlock Holmes. Studying law and philosophy. Keen, quick-witted, determined to make her uncle proud.

DR. MAXINE MORTIMER: A country doctor. Trustee- executrix of Sir Charles' will.

SIR HENRY BASKERVILLE: A distant relative from North America who recently inherited the Baskerville fortune.

JOHN STAPLETON: A naturalist living on the moor.

DOROTHEA STAPLETON: John Stapleton's sister...or maybe not.

BARRYMORE: Old family retainer at the Baskerville mansion.

MRS. BARRYMORE: Barrymore's wife.

HUGO BASKERVILLE: The family scoundrel. The cause of the curse. (may be doubled with Selden)

SIR CHARLES BASKERVILLE: A well-meaning philanthropist.

SELDEN: The lunatic brother of Mrs. Barrymore. (may be doubled with Hugo Baskerville)

LAURA LYONS: A young woman with a checkered past.

VICTORIA: LESTRADE: An eager young sleuth. (could be played by a man as VICTOR)

ASSORTED GROOMS, MAIDS, SHEPHERDS, HOUNDS, HENCHMEN and PEOPLE IN THE STREETS – The more the merrier!

TIME: 1889. October.

PLACE: London, England, and the Murky Moor of Devonshire.

SETTING:

The action of the play moves briskly from Sherlock Holmes' study at 221B Baker Street to a passenger railcar, to various rooms and corridors at Baskerville Hall and, of course, to the dark and mysterious Murky Moor beyond. The scenes should be sparsely furnished—a desk, a chair, a window frame and a drape or two here and there; a bench that serves as a railcar seat and so on. Lighting and sound effects will greatly aid in securing the locations in the minds of the audience. Space permitting, platforms and staircases could be used to considerable advantage. Whatever choices are made, scene changes should be executed in front of the audience and completed in the shortest time possible.

Note: *See Production Notes at the end of the script for additional staging options.*

BANNERS, SLIDES, SIGNS or POSTERS:

A series of banners/signs/slides or posters should be used to announce the upcoming scene or to reinforce the identity of a particular location.

COSTUMES, LIGHTS, PROPS, SOUND EFFECTS and MUSIC:

It is suggested that all actors and production personnel viewed by the audience—ushers and ticket takers alike—be costumed appropriately in the period (1870s-1880s). If full costuming is not possible, then signature items from the period such as assorted scarves, hats of all shapes and sizes, and long-sleeved shirts and vests will do nicely.

Lighting should establish a sense of the mysterious and the supernatural—shadows everywhere! Prop requirements for the show are few in number—a tea tray, a handbag, a revolver or two, a candle, a few ledgers and books, a suitcase here and there, that sort of thing.

Sound effects (SFX) should receive considerable attention. The use of onstage sound artists would be great fun! They should be surrounded by all the instruments and items needed to create the diverse and eerie sounds required in the show: the clip-clopping of horses' hooves on cobblestone streets; the sound of hissing steam spewing from a train engine; the howling wind as it races across the moor; as well as assorted moans, muffled screams and the like.

And, of course, of greatest importance is the horrendous and blood-curdling Sound of The Hound itself!

Music should be used to underscore transitions or set the emotional tone of a scene: high-pitched, staccato string arrangements; discordant percussion selections, dark and menacing. If possible, onstage musicians should be integrated into the aesthetic of the production.

A NOTE on the STYLE and PACING of the PRODUCTION:

Traditional time boundaries are often violated in this script. Flashback scenes, for example, are played as "movies" that are being watched by characters in the present tense. On occasion, characters from the present tense will talk with a "movie" character. In several scenes, they will also step into the "movie" reality and interact with "movie" characters. While the script identifies those moments where specific focus choices should be made, the director and cast may find additional moments that favor their distinctive production style.

Much of the comedy in the script is derived from an up-tempo, commedia-like pacing of the action. Quick, rapid-fire line delivery will help underscore the whacky nature of the text. At no time, however, should any action or set of lines overtly be "played for laughs." All characters must remain seriously engaged in solving the multiple mysteries the script contains. The comedy should derive from the incongruities between the real and the fanciful.

LINE ADDITIONS/DELETIONS:

In a few instances, lines of dialogue and/or stage directions have been placed between brackets [ ] to indicate they may be included or deleted depending on production and audience considerations.

At the CURTAIN:

Houselights and stagelights are up. Pre-show music is playing. Actors and crew members busy themselves putting the last few props in place, calling for a light check, hanging a backdrop or curtain swag. In short: revealing the "backstage" moments before the actual play begins.

As actors and crew members leave the set, stagelights and houselights begin to fade out. The period pre-show music segues into eerie, unsettling, supernatural sounds followed by a high-pitched, blood-curdling howl—the Sound of The Hound. It reverberates throughout the theater.

And then...the deep, labored breathing of Sir Charles Baskerville running for his life. "No, no, don't, don't! Someone help me!" The music and the Sound of The Hound come to a crescendo as the houselights go out. A spotlight keys on JENNIE WATSON.

ACT ONE

PROLOGUE

WATSON *(as the Sound of The Hound slowly dies away)*. Did you hear that blood-curdling wail? It chills me to the bone even now. And that desperate man running for his life! But wait, I'm getting ahead of myself. First things first. My name is Jennie Watson. The time: 1889. The place: London, England. A lovely Wednesday morning, or so I thought at the time. Stay close now. Don't wander off in the dark. There's so much more to come!

(SFX: The Sound of The Hound cracks through the theater. Then TRANSITION MUSIC kicks in—something Sherlock Holmes might enjoy.

LIGHTS out on WATSON as she exits and up on DR. MAXINE MORTIMER and SIR HENRY BASKERVILLE as they approach 221B Baker Street.)

SCENE 1 – WHERE'S SHERLOCK?

DR. MORTIMER. Hurry along, Sir Henry, there's not a moment to lose.

SIR HENRY. So, is this Sherlock Holmes fellow the right man for the job?

DR. MORTIMER. By all reputation, the very best. A brilliant mind, so I'm told. Ah, here we are.

(A SIGN/BANNER appears with "221B Baker Street" scrolled across it.

SFX: Door chime.

LIGHTS shift to Sherlock Holmes' study. A chair or two, a desk and a window frame covered by a heavy set of drapes. Several large books on philosophy and law are piled high on the desk. Behind them is SHIRLEY HOLMES loudly humming or playing a violin concerto. Assorted medical texts are strewn across the floor.

WATSON appears from the kitchen carrying a tray of tea and assorted tidbits.)

WATSON *(to AUDIENCE)*. As I mentioned a moment ago, it was a quiet Wednesday morning. Shirley and I were studying for our upcoming university exams. Yuck! I'd just finished making tea when the door chimed, rang, buzzed…whatever it is that door thingies do.

(SFX: Door chime.

WATSON sets down the tray and opens the door.)

WATSON *(cont'd)*. Yes?

DR. MORTIMER. Sherlock Holmes, please. Tell him Dr. Maxine Mortimer is here with Sir Henry Baskerville. And hurry!

SIR HENRY *(smiling at WATSON)*. Hi, there.

WATSON. Uh, yes, hi. Come in, please. *(To AUDIENCE.)* He had the prettiest eyes.

DR. MORTIMER. No flirting, young lady. We haven't much time.

SIR HENRY. My uncle Charles died mysteriously three months ago from the family curse.

WATSON. Good heavens!

DR. MORTIMER. Sir Henry arrived from North America yesterday to take over the family estate, so we're in a big hurry.

HOLMES *(popping her head up from behind that imposing pile of books)*. A family curse, did you say?

SIR HENRY. I did, yes. A curse from the past. The Hound of the Baskervilles.

(SFX: The Sound of The Hound!

EVERYONE does a "double take" as in "Did you hear something?")

WATSON. Shirley, did you hear anything?

HOLMES. Not quite sure.

DR. MORTIMER *(pushing forward)*. We need the brilliant mind of Sherlock Holmes this very instant! No time to waste.

HOLMES. Uncle Sherlock isn't here, I'm afraid. He's letting us use his flat while we're studying for our exams. I'm his niece, Shirley Holmes.

DR. MORTIMER. Did you say *Uncle* Sherlock?

WATSON. Yes, he's somewhere in Europe—Italy by now, I think—with another two months to go. He's with my uncle John.

DR. MORTIMER. *Uncle* John?

WATSON. Dr. John Watson, yes. They're colleagues, best friends, inseparable. I'm Jennie Watson. How do you do?

DR. MORTIMER. If the famous Sherlock Holmes isn't here, then who will solve this diabolical mystery?

HOLMES. Diabolical, did you say? Then perhaps we can help. Nothing like a diabolical mystery to tweak the imagination, eh, Jennie?

WATSON *(to AUDIENCE)*. Anything was better than studying for exams.

SIR HENRY. No offense, ladies, but this is a job for real detectives. Intelligent, strong. Afraid of nothing.

HOLMES. No offense taken, Sir Henry, but you're talking to the best and the brightest.

WATSON. He is?

HOLMES. As for intelligent, Jennie is studying to be a doctor like her famous uncle John.

WATSON. Indeed I am! And Shirley is studying logic and philosophy so she can follow in Uncle Sherlock's fabled footsteps.

HOLMES. And as for strong…well…

(HOLMES nods her head toward WATSON who masterfully puts SIR HENRY in a hammerlock. Or perhaps she executes a jujitsu hip roll or some other move that would catch the audience by surprise.)

WATSON *(releasing her grip)*. When it gets dark, bad things happen, Sir Henry. A girl has to be prepared.

SIR HENRY *(coughing, sputtering)*. Very impressive. Dr. Mortimer, let's give these little ladies a shot at the mystery, what do you think? Time is of the essence.

DR. MORTIMER. Well, if you're half as good as your uncles—

HOLMES. Trust me, Dr. Mortimer. It's all in the DNA.

DR. MORTIMER. The DNA, you say? What's that?

HOLMES. Another time perhaps, Dr. Mortimer. But first, the curse.

(LIGHTS dim down in Holmes' study.

Eerie MUSIC seeps its way under the scene.)

WATSON *(to AUDIENCE)*. Cold shivers ran up and down my arms! What were we getting ourselves into?

SCENE 2 – THE HUGO AFFAIR

(LIGHTS remain dim in Holmes' study as LIGHTS come up in the banquet room in Baskerville Hall.

A SIGN/BANNER appears with "Baskerville Hall—A Long Time Ago" scrolled upon it.

Revealed are HUGO BASKERVILLE—looking lovesick and depressed—and assorted HOUNDS, HENCHMEN, REVELERS, SQUIRES and WENCHES. Note: The char-

acters are as numerous and diverse as the director wishes them to be.

They are captured in a variety of frozen positions—gesturing, singing, [drinking, kissing], playing cards, wrestling, and so on.

HOLMES, WATSON, DR. MORTIMER and SIR HENRY watch HUGO and his HENCHMEN as if they are in a theater watching a "movie.")

DR. MORTIMER. It all began in 1742, one dark and shadowy night, when the vile and terrible Hugo Baskerville sat brooding with his henchmen in Baskerville Hall.

HOLMES. Is he the ugly, depressed, cruel-looking dude with a devilish sneer on his face?

DR. MORTIMER. How can you tell?

HOLMES. It's a talent.

DR. MORTIMER. Hugo had fallen in love with a local maiden. But she refused his advances.

(LIGHTS reveal the MAIDEN frozen in a "I refuse your advances" pose.)

MAIDEN. No, no, never!

DR. MORTIMER. But Hugo wouldn't take no, no, never for an answer.

HUGO. I cannot live without her! Bring her to me now!

(The HENCHMEN race "across town," grab the MAIDEN and race back to Baskerville Hall! WENCHS and others who are not involved cheer the HENCHMEN on.)

HUGO *(con't)*. Well done, lads! Put her in the upstairs room.

(The HENCHMEN plop the MAIDEN down in the up-stairs room and then return to the banquet room where everyone freezes once again, this time in advanced states of exhaustion.)

SIR HENRY. What a fiendish man.
DR. MORTIMER. The worst is yet to come.
WATSON. Oh, good!
HOLMES. Jennie?
WATSON. I mean…oh, bad, bad, very bad.
HUGO *(rising, a lecherous smile on his face)*. Be right back, boys. Time for my goodnight kiss. *(HUGO is about to enter the upstairs room.)*
WATSON *(to MAIDEN)*. Hurry! He's coming! Climb out the window. Grab the vine.

(A vine appears. The MAIDEN nods thanks to WAT-SON.)

WATSON *(con't)*. Good! Good! *(To HOLMES.)* Sorry, just came over me.

(The MAIDEN grabs the vine and climbs out the win-dow, escaping in the nick of time. But, alas, she has dropped a handkerchief behind. HUGO enters, sees the room is empty and spies the handkerchief on the floor.)

HUGO *(waving the handkerchief in the air)*. She has es-caped! Set the hounds upon her!

WATSON *(to AUDIENCE)*. Oh, oh, that doesn't sound so good!

(HUGO rubs the handkerchief over the nose of one of his HOUNDS.)

HUGO. Good boy! After her! My body and soul I give to the Powers of Evil if I can recapture my maiden!

(SFX: Assorted barks and yelps as the HOUNDS and HENCHMEN—on "horseback" now—begin to give chase.

A SIGN/BANNER appears with "The Dark and Murky Moor" scrolled upon it.

LIGHTS down in the banquet room and up on the Murky Moor, a place of rolling mists, frightening sounds and dark shadows...everywhere. And, on top of it all, rain is falling.

The movements described by DR. MORTIMER should be pantomimed in slow motion.)

DR. MORTIMER. It was a terrible night. Rain was falling. *(SFX)* The hounds were howling *(SFX)* and the horses were galloping across the moor *(SFX)*. Soon, Hugo and his hounds were out of sight. His henchmen lost the trail and asked two shepherds if they had seen Sir Hugo go by.

(LIGHTS key on the SHEPHERDS.)

SHEPHERD ONE. Hugo Baskerville passed us sitting high in the saddle upon his black mare. His eyes were crazed!
SHEPHERD TWO. And running behind him...

(Both SHEPHERDS fall to their knees.)

SHEPHERD ONE. ...was a massive hound of such evil proportions that we fell to our knees just like this and prayed to the saints for deliverance!

(SFX: The Sound of The Hound!

The SHEPHERDS and HENCHMEN respond to the howling, then look at HOLMES as if waiting for instructions.)

HOLMES. What are you looking at me for? Push on! Go! Go!

(LIGHTS out on the SHEPHERDS as the HENCHMEN are back in the chase.)

DR. MORTIMER. As Hugo's henchmen rode forward, their skins turned cold. Coming at them from out of the mist was Hugo's black mare *(SFX)*, running for its very life. But its saddle was empty.

(All the HENCHMEN follow the "mare" as it passes by. They are visibly shaken by the sight of the empty saddle.)

DR. MORTIMER *(con't)*. But, undaunted, they rode on. Soon they came upon the hounds...all whimpering *(SFX)* and cowering together.

(The HENCHMEN dismount, draw their pistols and cautiously gather at the edge of the stage where they peer into the "audience space.")

DR. MORTIMER *(con't)*. With their pistols raised...they slowly approached the rim of a small clearing where...in the cold light of the moon...the fair maiden had fallen dead from fear and fatigue.

HENCHMEN ADLIBS. The poor girl. Where's Hugo? It's creepy out here. [I want a beer!]

DR. MORTIMER. Then a sudden movement caught their eyes!

(The HENCHMEN gasp, scream!

MUSIC: Beast on the Murky Moor stuff!)

DR. MORTIMER *(con't)*. A great, black, foul thing, a beast shaped like a hound larger than any mortal eye has ever seen and its teeth were... [tearing out the throat of Hugo Baskerville!] ...it was a horrid sight to see...Hugo so dead and lifeless. Then the beast's red, blazing eyes turned upon Hugo's henchmen who shrieked with fear and rode away for dear life, screaming across the moor.

(SFX: Lots of screaming and a few frantic pistol shots as the HENCHMEN escape for their lives!

Note: The Hound itself should not be seen quite yet. Let the actors' reactions to the death of the MAIDEN and HUGO carry the moment.

LIGHTS down on the moor and up full in Holmes' study.)

WATSON *(to AUDIENCE)*. What a fantastic story! I could tell Shirley was as thrilled by the danger of it all as I was.

HOLMES *(restrained, always the steely-eyed professional)*. An amusing little fairy tale, Dr. Mortimer, but what does it have to do with Sir Henry?

SIR HENRY. Ever since that night, Miss Holmes, the men of Baskerville Hall have died in bloody, often mysterious ways.

HOLMES. Is that a fact?

DR. MORTIMER. Indeed. And then, a few months ago, poor Sir Charles took a late-night walk down his garden path.

WATSON *(to AUDIENCE)*. Ah! More pieces of the puzzle.

SCENE 3 – THE DEATH OF POOR SIR CHARLES

(As with the previous "movie" scene, LIGHTS remain dim in Holmes' study as LIGHTS come up on the garden at Baskerville Hall.

A SIGN/BANNER appears with "The Garden Late at Night" scrolled upon it.

It is nearly midnight. Large evergreen trees loom against the sky. A wicket-gate, four feet high at most, leads on to the Murky Moor. SIR CHARLES BASKERVILLE is revealed standing next to the gate. He is smoking a cigar.)

DR. MORTIMER. Each evening before bed, Sir Charles was in the habit of taking a walk around his garden.

SIR CHARLES. To stretch my legs. Smoke a cigar.

DR. MORTIMER. I told you about those cigars, Charles! With your heart palpitations and all.

SIR CHARLES. I know, dear Maxine, but with the bloody curse and everybody dying, well I needed something to calm my nerves.

(SFX: An unnerving sound draws SIR CHARLES' attention beyond the gate.)

SIR CHARLES *(cont'd)*. But wait! No, no. It can't be true.

SIR HENRY. What, Uncle Charles?

SIR CHARLES. No time to talk now…I have to… No! No! It can't be! No! *(SIR CHARLES drops his cigar and begins to run for his life down the gravel path. Note: Running in place, arms flailing, looking over his shoulder should do the trick nicely.)*

ADLIBS. What are you running from, Uncle Charles? Tell us! Careful there! Watch out for—

(SFX: Deep breathing, shoes running quickly across the gravel.

Suddenly SIR CHARLES—his face contorted, his fingers clawing the air, his spine curled back on itself—falls forward dead to the ground.)

SIR HENRY. Poor Uncle Charles.

(DR. MORTIMER steps into the garden scene and kneels next to SIR CHARLES.)

DR. MORTIMER. I was called to the garden about an hour after his body was discovered by Barrymore, the butler. Cardiac exhaustion. But that mask of horror on his face…I can't get it out of my mind.

(One by one, SIR HENRY, HOLMES and WATSON enter the garden as if entering a CSI crime scene.)

HOLMES. Careful, everyone. This is a crime scene. Watch where you're stepping. Did you notice anything out of the ordinary, Dr. Mortimer?

DR. MORTIMER. Yes. Over here, a few yards away from the body, I found more footprints.

WATSON. Footprints? Over there? *(Moving toward DR. MORTIMER.)* Where exactly, again?

(A bit disoriented by all the excitement, WATSON attempts to step over SIR CHARLES' body. But the garden is heavily in shadow and WATSON, instead, stumbles over the body, nearly falling to the ground. "Ooops, sorry!" she mutters under her breath while continuing on as if nothing has happened. Fortunately, no one observed her social blunder.

Note: See Production Notes regarding alternative "comic business.")

DR. MORTIMER. Footprints, yes, but not human prints.
SIR HENRY. Not human footprints? I don't think I like the sound of that.

(SIR HENRY, too, trips over his uncle in his enthusiasm to see inhuman footprints. "Sorry, Uncle Charles," he says as he continues on.

Simultaneously, while moving to where DR. MORTIMER is pointing, HOLMES can't help but trip over SIR CHARLES as well. She, too, mutters a lame apology and moves on.

Miraculously, both transgressions go undetected.)

HOLMES *(overlapping)*. Really, Dr. Mortimer, what are you saying? Not human footprints? Can it be so?
DR. MORTIMER. You're a city girl, Miss Holmes. You don't know how treacherous the moor can be. Shepherds have seen a huge creature, luminous, ghastly. A supernatural apparition spewing fire from its gaping jaws.
HOLMES. Supernatural? Keep it together, Dr. Mortimer. You're a woman of science.
DR. MORTIMER. The footprints were those of a…gigantic…hound, Miss Holmes! I know what I saw!

(SFX: The Sound of The Hound.

EVERYONE does a "double take" in an effort to determine the direction of the wailing they think they heard. In doing so, they end up not only stumbling over but stepping on SIR CHARLES as well!

They all mutter some apology under their breath. And again, miraculously, no one seems to notice anyone else's blunder.

All this tripping over his body, however, is too much for SIR CHARLES who "comes back to life" in an effort to determine from which direction the next assault might come!)

HOLMES. Paw prints, Dr. Mortimer? Is that what you're telling us? The prints of a—?

DR. MORTIMER. I am, yes. Forgive me. The terror on Sir Charles' face has unnerved me.

WATSON *(beginning to move toward the wicket-gate)*. Was that wicket-gate closed or open?

(As WATSON approaches him, SIR CHARLES successfully scoots out of her way. He is clearly pleased with himself.)

DR. MORTIMER. Closed and padlocked, yes.

WATSON. It's only four feet tall at the most. Anyone could have climbed over it, Holmes.

SIR HENRY *(giving WATSON an appreciative nod)*. Excellent, Miss Watson.

WATSON *(a bit flustered)*. Thank you, Sir Henry.

DR. MORTIMER. Sir Charles evidently stood by the gate for five or ten minutes, by the way. The ash had twice dropped from his cigar.

HOLMES. Outstanding, Dr. Mortimer. All right, everyone, one more look around before we move on, eh? Careful now!

(Fearing for his very life, metaphorically speaking, SIR CHARLES scoots this way and that, deftly avoiding every boot and shoe that comes his way as SIR HENRY, DR. MORTIMER, HOLMES and WATSON begin to leave the garden and return to Holmes' study.)

ADLIBS *(as necessary)*. Nothing more here, I don't believe. I can't see a thing. Is it always this foggy? This place needs some pruning. Anybody for a spot of tea?

(Finally, thinking he is safe at last, SIR CHARLES sits straight up and breathes a sigh of victory. But, alas, WATSON, who has been diligently peering at something or other, has not yet left the garden. But here she comes now!

Fear crosses SIR CHARLES' face. He tries to protect himself but, yes, alas again, WATSON manages to stumble over SIR CHARLES as she exits the garden and re-enters Holmes' study.)

WATSON *(not looking back, under her breath)*. Oh, dear, oh, dear, I am so, so sorry.

SIR CHARLES *(shaking his fist after WATSON)*. Watch where you're stepping next time, young lady! It's not easy being a dead body, you know?

(Then, in the best tradition of great melodramatic actors, SIR CHARLES gasps, flails his arms, claws the air and collapses into the position he originally fell into when he died the first time. Except this time he has one eye open and it's cocked at the thundering herd gathered in Holmes' study!

LIGHTS down on the garden and up full in Holmes' study.)

WATSON *(to AUDIENCE)*. Wow! That was exciting! And that howling thing? Pretty spooky stuff.

HOLMES *(to SIR HENRY)*. So, you're the last of the Baskervilles, eh?

DR. MORTIMER. Sir Charles never married. His brother, Rodger, the black sheep of the family and the spitting image of Sir Hugo, by the way, fled to South America. Never married, either. Died of yellow fever.

SIR HENRY. Sir Charles' younger brother, my father, died nearly twenty years ago.

HOLMES. But why do you want to reside at Baskerville Hall when all the men who live there meet with an evil fate?

SIR HENRY. Uncle Charles helped those less fortunate who lived in the region. I want to keep up his good works.

WATSON. That's very noble of you, Sir Henry.

SIR HENRY. That is, if I have a chance. *(SIR HENRY withdraws a crudely composed letter and hands it to HOLMES.*

(SFX: Mysterious, threatening, Phantom-of-the-Opera-type music.)

SCENE 4 – A THREATENING LETTER UNDER THE DOOR

(A SIGN/BANNER appears with "A Threatening Letter Under the Door" scrolled across it.)

SIR HENRY *(cont'd)*. It was under my door at the hotel this morning.

HOLMES *(reading the letter)*. "As you value your life or your reason, keep away from the moor!"

SIR HENRY. All cut out with scissors, I think. And glued onto the paper.

HOLMES. Jennie, quick! Yesterday's *Times*!

(WATSON begins looking for yesterday's Times.*)*

WATSON. It was just here a minute ago...where...found it!

DR. MORTIMER. Why are you reading yesterday's news-paper?

HOLMES. The inside page. The lead article! Read it, Jennie. Quickly!

WATSON. Looks like a boring piece about international trade or something...can't make heads or tails out of—

HOLMES. Jennie!

WATSON. Right. Sorry. Good. Yes. Here we go!

(As WATSON mentions the key words <u>underlined below</u>, they each should appear in full view. If fly space is plentiful, each word could be flown into the scene. Or an actor, or set of actors, could bring the words onstage or display each word on a tripod placed off to the side of the setting. Regardless of the display method, each word except the word moor should appear to have been "cut out" of The Times*. SIR HENRY and the others should relate to each word in an "ah, yes, I see now" fashion as they begin to understand how the threatening letter was created.)*

WATSON *(reading from the newspaper)*. "Although you may be flattered into thinking that your own special trade or your own industry will—

HOLMES. That gives us the words <u>you</u>, <u>your</u>, <u>or</u> and one more <u>your</u>! Now is the word value there?

WATSON. The word value? Uh...yes...here it is. "...diminish the <u>value</u> of..."

HOLMES *(overlapping)*. I need the word reason...see it there?

WATSON. Found it! "...it stands to <u>reason</u> that such..."

HOLMES. Now the words <u>keep</u> <u>away</u>...and <u>as</u>!

WATSON. Uh...yes, found them! See? And I found a <u>life</u>, too...all here, I think. Except...uh...moor...I can't find the word <u>moor</u>.

SIR HENRY *(as the word is displayed)*. It's written in longhand. Why, I wonder?

WATSON. It's not that common a word! Too much time to search throughout the entire edition.

HOLMES. Excellent, Jennie! The villain only had time to read the first article he found.

WATSON. Or she found.

HOLMES. Indeed, good point. We could be dealing with a fiendish woman.

DR. MORTIMER. Clever, indeed, whomever. *(As DR. MORTIMER reads the final sentence, the "words" arrange themselves so they spell out—)* "As you value your life or your reason, keep away from the moor!"

HOLMES *(to the "words," however they appeared on stage)*. Thanks very much. Excellent job all around.

ADLIBS *(as needed)*. Yes, indeed. Fine work. Thanks for stopping by.

(The "words" disappear.)

DR. MORTIMER. How did you know the words came from yesterday's *Times*?

HOLMES. The typeface used by the printer. No other paper uses it but *The Times*. Uncle Sherlock taught me that. And since Sir Henry just arrived yesterday, I deduced the words must have come from yesterday's *Times*.

DR. MORTIMER. Your uncle taught you well.

HOLMES *(pulling her thoughts together while moving to the window)*. So! Up to this point, we are dealing with an educated person—*The Times* is seldom found in the hands of the uneducated.

WATSON. But by cutting out simple, everyday words to compose the threat—

HOLMES. That individual wants us to think he or she is uneducated.

DR. MORTIMER. And that he or she feared his or her handwriting might be recognizable.

WATSON. Excellent grammar all around! Well done.

HOLMES *(peeking through the drapes)*. No time for grammar lessons, everyone. You've been followed.

SIR HENRY *(moving to the window)*. Followed?

HOLMES. No use! He's gone! A dark beard. Anyone living near Baskerville Hall have a full, black beard, Dr. Mortimer?

DR. MORTIMER. Sir Charles' butler, Barrymore. He has a full, black beard.

HOLMES. Did Barrymore profit at all by Sir Charles' will?

DR. MORTIMER. I don't know all the details of the estate yet, but—

HOLMES. A ballpark figure, Dr. Mortimer, please. How much is the entire estate worth?

DR. MORTIMER. Almost five million dollars!

(SFX: Whistles, wolf calls, and exclamations from EVERYONE available as they poke their heads around flats and door frames, even out of the lighting booth.)

EVERYONE IN UNISON. Five million bucks! What I could do with that!

(Then EVERYONE disappears. And all executed crisply, sharply, loudly and in about five seconds.

HOLMES and the others do a "double take.")

HOLMES. Yes, well! So! Someone or something doesn't want you to arrive at Baskerville Hall, Sir Henry. And we need to find out what's afoot. It's all very juicy, isn't it, Jenny?

WATSON. I can't wait.

HOLMES. You won't have to wait.

WATSON. I won't?

HOLMES. You leave on tonight's train for Baskerville Hall with Sir Henry and Dr. Mortimer.

WATSON. I do?

DR. MORTIMER. And not you, Miss Holmes?

HOLMES. I have some business to attend to here.

WATSON. What business?

HOLMES. Stuff 'n things. I have a hair appointment that I can't possibly change.

SIR HENRY. A hair appointment?

HOLMES. You have no idea how difficult it is to get a hair appointment, Sir Henry. Booked ahead for weeks! But never fear. Jennie's here.

WATSON. I am? Indeed, I am!

HOLMES. You'll send me letters by messenger as necessary. I'll join you when I can.

DR. MORTIMER. Thank you for your time.

SIR HENRY. Yes, my thanks to you both. See you on the train, Miss Watson.

(DR. MORTIMER and SIR HENRY exit. WATSON waves goodbye.)

HOLMES. You fancy Sir Henry, don't you, Jennie?

WATSON. Don't be silly. He is good looking though, don't you think?

HOLMES. Stay focused now, Jennie. Snoop around. Keep your eyes and ears open.

WATSON. I can't snoop around if I keep my eyes and ears closed, Shirley.

HOLMES. See? You're sharp as a tack already.

WATSON. But I don't think I can do this without you.

HOLMES. Of course you can. You've got Uncle John's pistol, don't you?

WATSON. It's in the closet. Top shelf. I'm a crack shot, too. Uncle John taught me.

HOLMES. You see, girlfriend, you're up to speed and ready to rumble! Be careful. It's an ugly business. Watch your back. Hurry now. You'll be late.

(WATSON and HOLMES hug goodbye.

LIGHTS out in Holmes' study as WATSON steps into a LIGHT POOL.)

WATSON *(to AUDIENCE)*. So there you have it. The excitement! The mystery! The Hound of the Baskervilles and…me! But surely I couldn't do it all without Shirley. Then again, maybe I could. I wanted to make Uncle John proud. And I couldn't do that if I sniveled and whined and made a complete boob of myself. So I packed as quickly as I could and made off for Victoria Station.

(LIGHTS out as WATSON exits.)

SCENE 5 – THE NIGHT RIDE TO BASKERVILLE HALL

(LIGHTS up on the interior of a railroad carriage—a simple bench will do with, perhaps, a window frame and curtains to embellish the setting.

A SIGN/BANNER appears with "Victoria Station" scrolled across it.

SFX: Crowd noises, hissing steam, general hustle and bustle associated with a crowded train station.

DR. MORTIMER and SIR HENRY are already in place. Their luggage is stacked nearby. WATSON enters hurriedly, suitcase in hand.)

SIR HENRY. Ah, here you are. Thought you might be late.

DR. MORTIMER *(overlapping)*. You all right, dear?

WATSON. All set. Fine. Terrible traffic is all. Couldn't find a cab.

SIR HENRY. Almost late myself. Couldn't find my old boots…the ones I wore on my sail across the ocean from America. Don't know how I could have misplaced them. Well, no matter now. I'm all set.

WATSON *(pulling a pistol from her handbag)*. So am I!

DR. MORTIMER. Look out!

(DR. MORTIMER ducks as WATSON waves the pistol around unconsciously.)

WATSON. Sorry. Just excited is all.

(SIR HENRY takes the pistol from WATSON who, sheepishly, opens her handbag. SIR HENRY places the pistol inside and smiles at WATSON.)

SIR HENRY. Welcome aboard, Miss Watson.
WATSON. Uh…yes…thank you.

(The train lurches forward. They all settle into the ride. DR. MORTIMER and SIR HENRY sit on either side of WATSON. All three move in unison—from side to side—to create the impression of a moving train.

SFX: The rhythmical, mechanical clacking of the wheels.

DR. MORTIMER and SIR HENRY look out their respective windows. After a beat or two…)

DR. MORTIMER. I think I'll rest my eyes for just a few moments…I've seen all this so many…
SIR HENRY. I really don't want to miss anything…but I'm so tired that…

(SIR HENRY and DR. MORTIMER are lulled to sleep by the movement of the train. As WATSON shares her thoughts with the AUDIENCE, the train leaves the city and penetrates the sparsely populated landscape.)

WATSON *(to AUDIENCE)*. How could they sleep? Such an adventure. And Sir Henry's favorite boots, remember? Going missing just before the trip? Was that a clue maybe? But a clue to what, I wondered?

(Strange LIGHTS play across their faces as darkness be-gins to fall. Things move in the dark, things we can't quite distinguish. The streets of London seem safe by comparison.)

WATSON *(cont'd)*. After a few hours, the brown earth had become all red and splotchy looking with thick grasses and ugly bushes everywhere. London was behind us. We were approaching the moor.

(The train lurches a bit. SIR HENRY and DR. MOR-TIMER come awake.)

SIR HENRY *(looking out his window)*. What is all that? Looks like something out of a nightmare.

(MUSIC and SFX: Something nightmarish!)

WATSON *(to AUDIENCE)*. In the distance—against the rising full moon—we could see a jagged hilltop all dim and grey and ominous.

DR. MORTIMER. Be always on your guard, Sir Henry. The moor is far more unforgiving and mysterious than your famous Rocky Mountains, I assure you.

SIR HENRY. Thank you, Dr. Mortimer, but I'm ready for whatever comes around the bend.

DR. MORTIMER. That's good to know, for we are almost there.

(SFX: Screeching wheels, the sound of steam pouring out of the exhausts, etc.

The windows disappear.

PERKINS enters the scene and stands behind the train seat which now serves as the seat of a horse-drawn carriage. The luggage remains stacked where it was.)

PERKINS. Evening, Dr. Mortimer.

DR. MORTIMER. Perkins.

PERKINS. I can tell you're Sir Henry, sir. But this pretty lady?

WATSON. Jennie Watson.

PERKINS. A pleasure, Jennie Watson. You'll be sparking things up around here, I suspect.

SIR HENRY. Mind your manners, sir.

PERKINS. No offense intended, Gov'nor. Having my fun is all. OK, folks. Hang on tight. We're off!

(PERKINS extends his hands as if holding the reins to several horses.

LIGHTS change. We are on the winding road to Baskerville Hall. This ride is considerably bumpier than the train trip, harrowing in fact!

SIR HENRY, WATSON and DR. MORTIMER are tossed to and fro. PERKINS, who knows each dip and furrow on the road, remains upright and confident.

EVERYONE raises their voices to be heard over the clatter of the journey. Assorted groans and gasps punctuate the trip.

Note: From this point on, both SFX and MUSIC should play an exceedingly important role in the production. Find places to accent a line, or a key word or two. Be subtle or blatant as the scene requires. Have fun with the challenge of it all!)

PERKINS *(cont'd)*. I need to warn you good people. Be aware. A convict escaped from the asylum three days ago.

WATSON. A convict?

SIR HENRY. From an asylum, did you say?

PERKINS. Yep. Nuttier than a fruitcake!

WATSON. What did he do?

PERKINS. They say he robbed and murdered three people! So keep your eyes peeled, eh? *(Pulling back hard on the reins.)* Whoa! We're here. Welcome home, Sir Henry. Watch your step.

(LIGHTS shift. We have arrived at the gates of Baskerville Hall.

A SIGN/BANNER appears with "Mysterious Baskerville Hall" scrolled across it.

Gloomy ivy hangs everywhere. Granite walls rise out of sight. Arches, leaves and rotted things abound—anything to give the impression that the structure is on its last legs.

BARRYMORE and MRS. BARRYMORE meet the travelers. BARRYMORE has a full, dark black beard.)

BARRYMORE. Good evening, Dr. Mortimer. Arrived safely, I see.

DR. MORTIMER. Barrymore, this is Sir Henry Baskerville.

BARRYMORE. An honor, Sir Henry. Welcome to Baskerville Hall.

DR. MORTIMER. And this young lady is—

WATSON *(like an eager puppy)*. Jennie Watson. Hi. Very pleased to meet you.

DR. MORTIMER. She'll be a guest of the Hall for a few days.

BARRYMORE. My wife. Elizabeth.

(Nods and greetings all around. MRS. BARRYMORE remains aloof.)

BARRYMORE *(cont'd)*. You must all be tired. Hot tea in your rooms shortly. Perkins, give me a hand here.

(BARRYMORE and PERKINS busy themselves with the luggage. MRS. BARRYMORE exits to prepare WATSON's room.)

SIR HENRY. So, the family home at last. Needs a little sprucing up. I'll get right on that as soon as we deal with this Baskerville hound problem.

WATSON *(whispering to DR. MORTIMER and SIR HENRY)*. Did you see how cold Mrs. Barrymore looked? Didn't even shake my hand. And Barrymore has a full, black beard.

SIR HENRY. Just like the man we saw through Holmes' window.

DR. MORTIMER *(seeing PERKINS and BARRYMORE return)*. Perkins? Let's be off. I'm exhausted. Good night, Barrymore. And remember, Sir Henry! The moor! Be ever watchful!

(LIGHTS shift as DR. MORTIMER and PERKINS exit and SIR HENRY, WATSON and BARRYMORE enter the interior of Baskerville Hall.

This area will serve a variety of locations in Baskerville Hall. And while a stone archway or two, as well as a stone fireplace, would add much to the feel of an old castle, a few chairs, a serviceable table and a hanging drape over a window frame or two will be sufficient.

That said, it is important that a portrait of Hugo Baskerville be visible. More on his exact features later. If possible, other portraits of severe, dour, unhappy-looking old men may be displayed...all family members from a bygone era.)

SIR HENRY *(looking at the portrait[s])*. Who is that gloomy looking guy hanging on the wall?
BARRYMORE *(entering with the tea)*. Your ancestor, Sir Henry. Hugo Baskerville himself.
WATSON. Ah, the cause of it all, eh?

[If more portraits are visible, add the following line.

BARRYMORE. And there, poor man, on the right, is your uncle Charles.]

SIR HENRY. Tomorrow I want to see where Uncle Charles died, Barrymore, and I'll need to look at his records, his important papers, everything.

BARRYMORE. As you wish, Sir Henry.

(SFX: The Sound of The Hound! But closer now, a heart-splitting howl-scream-moan that brings to mind the tortured wail of a dying beast.)

SIR HENRY. Good heavens, what was that?

BARRYMORE. It's almost a nightly occurrence, Sir Henry. Some say it comes from another world.

WATSON. And what do you say, Barrymore?

BARRYMORE. I say don't leave the house after dark, Miss Watson. Never. Are you ready, Sir Henry?

SIR HENRY. Yes. Well, enough for one day. Good night, Miss Watson. Sleep well if you can.

(BARRYMORE and SIR HENRY exit.

Lights fade as WATSON steps into a LIGHT POOL.)

WATSON *(overlapping their exit)*. I agree. Excellent idea. I'm bushed, too, whipped, nothing left in the tank.

WATSON *(cont'd., to AUDIENCE)*. Alone at last. Had to make some notes! *(Withdraws paper and a writing instrument from her handbag.)* "Shirley: Mrs. Barrymore is a bit creepy. Perkins is a classic 'Bad Boy,' but he did pay me a nice compliment. Oh, yeah, Sir Henry thinks someone stole his boots, and Barrymore has a black beard. More later." *(To AUDIENCE.)* And that wailing thing a moment ago? Was that the lunatic? Or was it something worse, maybe? I was afraid that I wouldn't be good enough for the job. And then…

(SFX : The sob of a woman, the muffled, strangling gasp of one who is torn by an uncontrollable sorrow. It fills the damp and chilly corridors of Baskerville Hall, and echoes throughout the theater.)

WATSON *(cont'd)*. Hear that? Kept me up most of the night! I tossed and turned but I couldn't… *(SFX: Wind, lots of wind!)* And the wind! What was I doing here? Where was Shirley when I needed her? I finally dozed off a bit. Then boom! It was morning!

SCENE 6 – THE MORNING AFTER THE NIGHT BEFORE

(LIGHTS come up full in the breakfast room at Baskerville Hall. WATSON's LIGHT POOL fades out.

A SIGN/BANNER appears with "The Morning After the Night Before" scrolled across it.

SIR HENRY is looking out across the moor. BARRYMORE is pouring the tea.)

WATSON *(cont'd., to AUDIENCE while moving into the scene)*. Well, here I go. Shirley or no Shirley. *(To SIR HENRY.)* Morning, Sir Henry, Barrymore.
BARRYMORE *(handing WATSON a cup of tea)*. Good morning, Miss Watson.

WATSON. Whoa, what a night, eh, Sir Henry? All that wind!

SIR HENRY *(with a sense of urgency and concern)*. Miss Watson? Did you hear something last night? A woman, perhaps?

WATSON. A woman? Last night?

SIR HENRY. Yes, a woman sobbing in the night.

WATSON. Sobbing? Yes! Kept me up most of the—

BARRYMORE *(interrupting)*. A dream most likely, Sir Henry. Sleep is often fitful on the moor.

(MRS. BARRYMORE enters. She busies herself with cups and saucers. SIR HENRY and WATSON watch her closely.)

WATSON. Good morning, Mrs. Barrymore.

MRS. BARRYMORE *(averting her face)*. Morning, Miss Watson.

WATSON. Sleep well?

MRS. BARRYMORE. As well as can be expected, miss, what with the chill in the air—

SIR HENRY. And a lunatic on the loose.

(For a moment it appears MRS. BARRYMORE might burst into tears. Then she runs from the room.)

WATSON. Is Mrs. Barrymore all right?

BARRYMORE. The shock and strain of Sir Charles' death is all. Now then, if there won't be anything else, I have work to be done. *(BARRYMORE bows and then exits.)*

WATSON. Did you see her eyes? All red? Bloodshot? Hadn't slept a wink. Something's off here. Watch your back, Sir Henry.

SIR HENRY. Thanks for your concern, Miss Watson.

WATSON *(a bit flustered by SIR HENRY's attention)*. Don't want anything to happen to you, do we? You being our first client and all. Wouldn't do much for future business if you ended up dead.

SIR HENRY. Point well taken. OK, time to get crackin'. I'm off to Sir Charles' study. More later. *(SIR HENRY exits.)*

WATSON *(to AUDIENCE)*. I think he likes me. Just a little. Don't you think so? The way he tilts his head to the left? So cute.

(SFX: Murky Moor sounds. Wind building up.)

WATSON *(cont'd., acknowledging the SFX)*. But no time for romance now. Off to see the terrain. Firsthand detective stuff.

SCENE 7 – THE MURKY MOOR UP CLOSE AND PERSONAL

(LIGHTS down in the breakfast room and up on the Murky Moor.

A SIGN/BANNER appears with "The Murky Moor Up Close and Personal" scrolled across it.

SFX: Lots and lots of Murky Moor stuff!)

WATSON *(to AUDIENCE)*. A walk across the moor is no picnic, let me tell you. The smells? Pee-yew! Wet stuff all over the place and bubbling pools of—

STAPLETON *(offstage)*. Stop! Don't take another step!

(WATSON stops mid-step as STAPLETON enters, hoisting a tin box for botanical specimens over one shoulder and waving a green butterfly net in an effort to capture WATSON's attention.)

STAPLETON. Not there! Watch your every step, young lady. Or you'll be lost forever.

WATSON. Thank you for the warning.

STAPLETON. One false step yonder means death to man or beast. Only yesterday I saw a horse wander into it. Didn't have a chance, poor animal. Sucked into the muck in a matter of seconds.

WATSON. How ghastly! This must be an awful place!

STAPLETON. They don't call it the Murky Moor for nothing.

WATSON. And what do they call you, sir?

STAPLETON. Oh, so sorry. Yes. John Stapleton. I am a naturalist in search of botanical species of infinite beauty and variety. I know every trail in and out of the moor.

WATSON. A pleasure to meet you. My name is—

STAPLETON. Jennie Watson. Yes, I know. Your uncle is Dr. John Watson, famous surgeon and companion to the really, really famous Sherlock Holmes. Dr. Mortimer and I are good neighbors. We were having tea with Maxine this morning, you see?

WATSON. Yes, well, who might we be, exactly?

(DOROTHEA STAPLETON enters, carrying a small wrapped package in her hand. She is a bit on edge. She doesn't see WATSON at first.)

MISS STAPLETON. John? You forgot your lunch...oh, hello.

STAPLETON *(making introductions)*. My sister, Dorothea. This is Jennie Watson, my dear. Maxine mentioned her.

MISS STAPLETON. Hello. Yes. Very nice to meet you.

STAPLETON. And so you've come to investigate the shocking death of Sir Charles. Too bad the fabulous duo couldn't make it instead. But I'm sure you'll do your best.

WATSON *(retrieving paper again, taking notes)*. Did you know Sir Charles well?

MISS STAPLETON. Oh, yes. Most charming. His favorite walk was over the moor to our house.

STAPLETON. For good company and conversation. I had a school in the North country. Helping to mold young minds. Very satisfying. Sir Charles was a great supporter of education.

MISS STAPLETON. But the fates were against us.

WATSON. Oh? What fates might those have been, exactly?

STAPLETON. A serious epidemic broke out in the school.

MISS STAPLETON. Three of the boys died.

WATSON *(scribbling frantically)*. ...Three...boys...died. Oh, dear!

STAPLETON. The school never recovered. But my love of nature sustains me. I have the most complete collection of Lepidoptera in the entire southwest of England.

(A SIGN/BANNER appears with "Lepidoptera? What's that?" scrolled across it.

At the same time EVERYONE available pops their heads out from wherever they are.)

EVERYONE *(in unison, enunciating each syllable).* Lep-i-dop-tera? What's that?

STAPLETON. Butterflies and moths, my dear Miss Watson. *(Sarcastically.)* Your uncle would have known that.

EVERYONE. Oh, oh, look out for him, Jennie! *(EVERYONE magically disappears!)*

MISS STAPLETON *(playing peacemaker).* You must stay for dinner, Miss Watson. Please. I insist.

WATSON. You're too kind but I must get back to Sir Henry. There's much to—

(SFX: A low moan, indescribably sad, sweeps over the moor.)

WATSON. Did you hear that?

STAPLETON. Just the mud settling. Gurgling. Nothing to worry about.

WATSON. That was no gurgle, Mr. Stapleton. It was a living, breathing sound!

STAPLETON. The moor plays tricks on your senses, Miss Watson. That's all you're hearing. The sound of fear. It's safer for you in London. *(Seeing a butterfly.)* Oh, a Cyclopides! That's a butterfly to you, Miss Watson. Come to dinner soon! Bye-bye! *(STAPLETON runs after the butterfly.)*

WATSON. Well, nice to have met you, Miss—

MISS STAPLETON *(urgently)*. Go back, Miss Watson. Quickly!

WATSON. Yes, well, I was just about to—

MISS STAPLETON. London! Go back to London! This instant. And take Sir Henry with you. Get away from this place now!

WATSON. But we must discover how Sir Charles—

MISS STAPLETON. You silly girl. Believe me. It is imperative. You must leave now!

WATSON. I'm not a silly girl. Make no mistake about it. And I am determined to—

MISS STAPLETON. You are in danger, Miss Watson. Be watchful! *(MISS STAPLETON exits, running.)*

(LIGHTS down on the moor as WATSON steps into a LIGHT POOL.)

WATSON *(to AUDIENCE)*. Did you see the look of fear in her eyes? She knows something. And what about Stapleton's snotty tone? *(Mispronouncing.)* Lepidop... ter...a! Please! Who can possibly care about some silly old butterflies when there are dead bodies thither and yon? And that moaning sound? But wait, wait! There's more! Later that night, when I'm almost asleep...

SCENE 8 – FOOTSTEPS DOWN THE HALL

(LIGHTS up on the corridor outside WATSON's bed-room. WATSON's LIGHT POOL fades out.

A SIGN/BANNER appears with "Footsteps Down the Hall" scrolled across it.

BARRYMORE is moving down the corridor. He's hold-ing a small, flickering candle.)

WATSON *(cont'd)*. I hear footsteps approaching my bed-room door! I don't move a muscle. I pull the blankets tight up to my neck. The footsteps stop just outside the door! Then, after a moment, they continue down the hall What should I do? What would Shirley do?

(LIGHTS UP on HOLMES in a tight LIGHT POOL. She is "inside" WATSON's brain, serving as a mentor-cheerleader urging WATSON to be courageous.

HOLMES speaks directly to WATSON. WATSON contin-ues addressing the AUDIENCE but never acknowledges HOLMES' presence.)

HOLMES. I'd follow the flickering candle, Jennie. That's what I'd do. Not too close. Not too far.
WATSON. Yes, of course you would. You'd get out of bed. You wouldn't hide under the covers like a wimpy girl.
HOLMES. Absolutely not!

(WATSON opens the bedroom door slowly and peeks out.)

WATSON. And you'd open the door, peek out.

HOLMES. The light, Jennie! Follow the light.

WATSON. And look down the hallway.

HOLMES. Don't lose the light!

WATSON. A man, I think, Barrymore, perhaps. In shirt and trousers with no covering on his feet. He doesn't want to be heard!

HOLMES. But you heard him!

WATSON. But I heard him, I did, indeed.

HOLMES. Excellent work!

WATSON. So I begin stalking the shadowy figure.

(BARRYMORE and WATSON animate the details of the action.)

WATSON *(cont'd)*. My heart's pounding in my chest. Am I going to be caught? How do I explain wandering Baskerville Hall in my nightgown? I stay so far behind the figure that I think I've lost him. But then I catch a thin glimmer of light through a barely open door. There, do you see it?

HOLMES. I do, yes. Good girl.

WATSON. I tiptoe closer, peek inside the room. Barrymore's holding a candle high up against the window. Then he lets out a deep groan and blows out the candle.

HOLMES. Careful now!

WATSON. I press myself into the shadows as he hurriedly passes me by and disappears down the hallway.

(BARRYMORE exits.)

HOLMES. That was close!

WATSON. I return to my room and as I'm about to slip into bed...

(SFX: The loud, metallic clang of a metal key turning in an old, rusty lock.)

HOLMES. What was that?

WATSON. A key turning somewhere in Baskerville Hall. But where? I could not tell. There was some secret business going on in this house of gloom, and I was determined to find the cause of it all.

HOLMES. But you were stressing out.

WATSON. But I was stressing out! I feared I was in over my head. I needed Shirley's help.

HOLMES. Write me a letter, girlfriend. I can't wait!

WATSON. And I did, too! And when you all return from intermission, we'll show you what happened next. Hurry back. The Hound awaits!

(SFX: The Sound of The Hound!

MUSIC up.

LIGHTS out!)

INTERMISSION

ACT TWO

PROLOGUE

(SFX and MUSIC signify that all is about to resume.

LIGHTS down in the theater and up on WATSON standing in a LIGHT POOL.)

WATSON *(to AUDIENCE)*. OK! Everyone back? Excellent. We're all set to go. But first, let's have a quick review.

(As WATSON highlights the action so far, LIGHTS should capture the key individuals mentioned in representative poses. SFX and MUSIC should cap off each revelation with a snappy sound or a blast of a horn of some sort. It should all move swiftly, of course, much like a quick-cutting movie trailer seeking to whet our appetite for more!

Time and personnel permitting, it might be fun to drop in the various SIGNS/BANNERS used as guideposts throughout Act One.)

WATSON *(cont'd)*. It all began with the chiming, ringing, buzzing…that something or other with the door ringer, remember?

(SFX: Door chime.)

WATSON *(cont'd)*. And then Jennie and I met Dr. Mortimer and Sir Henry, and we all watched as the poor maiden tried to escape!

(DR. MORTIMER, SIR HENRY and HOLMES as they witness the MAIDEN in her "No, no" pose, and HUGO and HENCHMEN "on horseback" giving chase.)

WATSON *(cont'd)*. Followed by the gripping death of Sir Charles…

(SIR CHARLES in his signature "it was so painful" pose.)

WATSON *(cont'd)*. Then that bumpy ride to Baskerville Hall where we met Barrymore and his standoffish wife.

(BARRYMORE, bowing and subservient, and MRS. BARRYMORE, suspicious and resentful.)

WATSON *(cont'd)*. And that awful Stapleton man with his snotty manners and his frightened-looking sister, and all those goopy-sounding sounds of the moor.

(STAPLETON, condescending and superior, and MISS STAPLETON, furtive and frightened. SFX: Lots of goopy-sounding sounds!)

WATSON *(cont'd)*. And not a wink of sleep because of the wind and Barrymore's footsteps down the hall…and through it all…

(SFX: The Sound of The Hound!

As the Sound of The Hound fills the theater, all the characters disappear, the LIGHTS onstage go down. All that is left is WATSON in a tight LIGHT POOL.)

WATSON *(cont'd)*. Yep, I think that about does it. OK. Now, when last we met, I was at my wit's end and needed to fill Shirley in on all that had happened. So, during the intermission, I wrote Shirley a letter and gave it to a messenger who jumped on the morning train…

(WATSON whips out paper, a writing utensil and an envelope.

As WATSON continues with her dialogue, a MESSEN-GER suddenly appears, snatches the envelope out of WATSON's hand and rides the train to London (SFX) where he negotiates several crowded streets (SFX) before delivering it to 221B Baker Street.)

WATSON *(cont'd)*. …ran through the fabled streets of London…

(Note: It might be fun to people these fabled streets with shoving strollers, tradesmen, pushcart sellers and the like. They should all appear as quickly as possible, all shouting and gesturing and creating a horrendous sea of sound and bodies through which the MESSENGER must navigate before arriving, exhausted, at 221B Baker Street.

LIGHTS up on HOLMES in her uncle's study.)

WATSON *(cont'd)*. And delivered the letter to Shirley!

(SFX: Door chime.

As soon as the MESSENGER arrives, the street people disappear.

HOLMES answers the door, takes the letter, and offers a tip to the MESSENGER.)

HOLMES. Thank you so very much, my good—

(The MESSENGER snatches HOLMES' tip out of her hand, takes a deep breath, looks apprehensively down the street, and cautiously begins the dangerous journey back to the train station. Perhaps, however, on this occasion the MESSENGER is lucky enough to encounter no one at all.

Or...

The London hordes have not disappeared at all. Instead, they eagerly anticipate the MESSENGER's return! But maybe this time the MESSENGER decides to jump into a pushcart and be chauffeured to the train! Or several of the street people might attack the poor MESSENGER, stealing a coat and both shoes. Or perhaps, a flirtation could occur and the MESSENGER quickly loses all interest in catching the next train back to the moors!

Whatever decisions are made concerning the MESSEN-GER's journey, these "bits" should take no more than ten seconds—the quicker, the cleaner, the better!

The MESSENGER, of course, with strong SFX support, could make the journey solo, simply pantomiming everything along the way.

From this point on in the scene, HOLMES and WATSON talk to each other.)

HOLMES *(referring to the letter)*. Gurgling swamps. Snot-nosed butterfly catchers and escaped lunatics! Barrymore and the lighted candle! So vivid I felt I was right there with you.

WATSON. But you're not! You're there and I'm here. There's too much for one person to keep up with. And then there's that goofy love stuff.

HOLMES. What goofy love stuff?

WATSON *(pointing toward the moor)*. That stuff!

SCENE 1 – THAT GOOFY LOVE STUFF

(LIGHTS dim down on HOLMES and come up on SIR HENRY and MISS STAPLETON walking on a path through the moor.

A SIGN/BANNER appears with "That Goofy Love Stuff" scrolled across it.

WATSON observes the scene but hangs back a distance. SIR HENRY and MISS STAPLETON are in intimate discussion, her arm entwined in his. She smiles, laughs, looks up at him. It is clear they are comfortable in each other's presence.)

HOLMES. No! Oh, poor Jennie. I'm so sorry.

WATSON. And I thought he liked me, too. Men! Oh, well, so, I'm on my way to Dr. Mortimer's house a few days ago, and there they were, just like that, cheek to cheek.

HOLMES. So you spied on them. Good for you. Tell all!

(SIR HENRY and MISS STAPLETON dramatize the actions WATSON describes.)

WATSON. OK! So she's smiling, he's smiling. Then Sir Henry puts his arm around Miss Stapleton's waist and whispers in her ear. He's about to kiss Miss Stapleton but then she pushes him away and says—

MISS STAPLETON. Your life is at stake, Sir Henry! Leave Baskerville Hall tonight! Save yourself!

WATSON. Then Sir Henry says—

SIR HENRY. I am captivated by your presence. I will not leave unless you leave with me!

WATSON. He's about to kiss her just as snotty face enters the scene waving that silly looking butterfly net like a madman.

ADLIBS *(interspersed throughout)*. What are you doing with—? Now, John, please! Your sister and I—! Don't you ever—! I have no intention of—!

WATSON. Miss Stapleton pushes Sir Henry away. Snotty face leaps around like a nut case. Sir Henry can't get a word in. Then snotty face points in the direction of their house and Miss Stapleton runs off, crying. Snotty face gives Sir Henry a mean look and then runs off after his sister!

(MISS STAPLETON and STAPLETON exit.)

WATSON *(cont'd)*. Poor Sir Henry. His shoulders go all droopy. He hangs his head and starts walking back to Baskerville Hall.

(SIR HENRY exits.

LIGHTS fade down on the moor and come up slowly in the breakfast room at Baskerville Hall.)

HOLMES. Well, that was exciting.
WATSON *(as she moves into the breakfast room)*. Wait, wait, there's more!
HOLMES. Oh, goody! More intrigue.

(LIGHTS up full in the breakfast room.

A SIGN/BANNER appears with "Another Boring Breakfast of Tea and Scones...What Are Scones, Anyway?" scrolled across it.

WATSON enters the scene while still addressing HOLMES. SIR HENRY is having his morning tea.)

WATSON. The next morning at breakfast, Sir Henry launches into his side of the story like a lovesick puppy!

SIR HENRY. Behaving like a crazy man, he was, Miss Watson.

WATSON. Is that so?

SIR HENRY. And all because of Dorothea! I've only known her these few weeks, Miss Watson, but I feel she's the woman for me.

WATSON. How nice for you.

SIR HENRY. There's a light in a woman's eyes that speaks louder than words, you know?

WATSON. I'll keep that in mind.

HOLMES. Watch it, Jennie.

SIR HENRY. She must know how I feel, but she keeps warning me to leave Baskerville Hall. Then, as I'm about to kiss her, Stapleton bumbles into the scene. What are my intentions for his sister? And being the Lord of the Manor doesn't give me the right to barge into their lives.

WATSON. But you protested.

SIR HENRY. I certainly did. I told him I had strong feelings for Dorothea. That I was not ashamed of my emotions.

WATSON. Never!

SIR HENRY. That I hoped she might honor me by becoming Mrs. Baskerville.

WATSON *(disappointed)*. Oh, my! How nice for her. Then he ordered Miss Stapleton home, I suspect, and you were left all alone, confused, shoulders drooping.

SIR HENRY. Yes! It's almost as if you were there.

WATSON. A woman's intuition is all we need, Sir Henry.

SIR HENRY *(an idea taking root in his mind)*. Indeed! You're an attractive young woman, Miss Watson.

WATSON. Why, thank you.

SIR HENRY. Intelligent. Energetic. Adventuresome.

WATSON. How nice of you to notice.

SIR HENRY. Is there anything that would prevent me from making a good husband to a woman that I loved? Tell me the truth. Both barrels. I can take it.

HOLMES. Oh, oh.

WATSON *(blushing a bit too much perhaps)*. I think not, Sir Henry. No, nothing at all. You're strong. Courageous. Nice smile. Straight teeth.

SIR HENRY. But she wouldn't let me kiss her. Why? Bad breath, perhaps? Oh, dear, do I have bad breath?

WATSON. Bad breath? Let me see, if you don't mind. Go ahead. Remember, I'm a professional. *(WATSON lifts her face up to SIR HENRY's and closes her eyes.)*

HOLMES. Jennie, what are you doing?

SIR HENRY. Well, it's most irregular. But, as you say, it's all professional.

(SIR HENRY leans down as if to kiss WATSON but, instead, "poofs" his breath into her face. WATSON pulls away, coughs slightly, then smiles at SIR HENRY.)

WATSON. A rose by any other name, Sir Henry, would smell as sweet. Your breath is…lovely.

SIR HENRY. Oh, thank you. I feel better now. I'm still in the running then! You've been wonderful about this goofy love stuff, Miss Watson.

WATSON. Thank you.

SIR HENRY. You're quite a girl! Like the little sister I never had. *(Hugging her in a brotherly fashion.)* Well, I'm off to learn more about Sir Charles' estate. Be safe.

(SIR HENRY exits with great energy while WATSON seems to wilt.

LIGHTS out in the breakfast room as WATSON steps into a LIGHT POOL.)

WATSON *(to AUDIENCE)*. His little sister! Did you hear that? He doesn't even know I exist. This is all too much for me. *(To HOLMES.)* Oh, by the way, Shirley, I forgot. Stapleton knows all about us.

HOLMES. He does? How?

WATSON. Dr. Mortimer flapped her yap when she was having breakfast with the Stapletons a few days ago. He wants to meet you. Learn all about famous Uncle Sherlock!

HOLMES. All in good time. But now I've got to be going. Keep the letters coming, Jennie. *(LIGHTS slowly fade down on HOLMES.)*

WATSON. Wait! Don't leave me. Not yet. I need your help! Shirleeeeyyyy!

(LIGHTS out on HOLMES.)

WATSON *(cont'd., to AUDIENCE)*. Where is she going now? I'm drowning here! I'm falling in love with Sir Henry, who's falling in love with Miss Stapleton. And then there's snotty face…something mucho weirdo is going on with that guy. Then the rain and the thunder kick in, and that mist stuff coming out of nowhere, and the sounds and the screams! It's a nightmare!

(SFX: A rousing symphony of all kinds of sounds and groans and screams come from everywhere.

Then, as suddenly as they arrived, the sounds and groans and screams are gone. All that remain are the sounds of rain and thunder.)

WATSON *(cont'd).* Hear what I mean? And then when Barrymore did another candle thing, I just had to write Shirley another letter!

(WATSON pulls an envelope out of her handbag and waves it in the air.

The MESSENGER appears once again, takes the envelope and repeats the journey from Baskerville Hall to London that we witnessed earlier.

Note: *If tradesmen, pushcart sellers and the like appear again, the MESSENGER should try valiantly to defend him/herself and the letter! Perhaps by going on the offensive, as if carrying a football downfield—stiff-arming people out of the way! Exhausted, the MESSENGER arrives at 221B Baker Street.*

SFX: Door chime.

LIGHTS up in Holmes' study. HOLMES appears, takes the letter, tips the MESSENGER and watches as the MESSENGER summons up the energy to rejoin the teeming fray.

Perhaps, this time, however, the MESSENGER flees through the theater, thus avoiding any confrontation with street people altogether!)

HOLMES *(opening the letter)*. So what do we have this time, eh? Moans and howls and the Murky Mist of the Moor. You're having way too much fun! I'm all ears. Go!

SCENE 2 – BARRYMORE DOES THAT CANDLE THING AGAIN

(LIGHTS dim down on HOLMES while shifting to the dark hallways of Baskerville Hall. BARRYMORE appears dressed as he did the first time. With him on this occasion, however, is MRS. BARRYMORE. They move down the hallway.)

WATSON *(to HOLMES)*. A few nights ago I heard Barrymore's footsteps coming down the hall again. But someone else was with him. So after they passed my door I knocked on Sir Henry's door! *(SFX)* Sir Henry? Get up. Quick!
HOLMES. Excellent.

(SIR HENRY appears, a bit disheveled but ready for an adventure.

WATSON and SIR HENRY follow BARRYMORE and MRS. BARRYMORE down the hallway.

MUSIC and SFX: Sneaking down the hall stuff!

At one point, MRS. BARRYMORE hears a sound (SFX) and turns quickly. WATSON and SIR HENRY are caught off guard and press themselves back into the shadows. Has MRS. BARRYMORE seen them?)

HOLMES. Careful, Jennie!
MRS. BARRYMORE. What was that noise, Mr. Barrymore?
BARRYMORE *(turning toward the sound he thinks he heard)*. I don't rightly know, Mrs. Barrymore. Let's give a listen.

(WATSON's nose is almost touching BARRYMORE's.)

WATSON *(whispering to AUDIENCE)*. I could tell the Barrymores had sausage for supper...with garlic! Yuck!

(Fortunately, BARRYMORE, seeing nothing out of the ordinary, continues down the hall. MRS. BARRYMORE follows, as do WATSON and SIR HENRY. They enter the same room BARRYMORE entered previously. BARRYMORE raises the candle up to the window and moves it back and forth across the glass.

SIR HENRY and WATSON burst into the room.)

SIR HENRY. What are you doing with that candle, Barrymore?
BARRYMORE. Checking the windows, Sir Henry.

MRS. BARRYMORE *(overlapping)*. Being sure we're safe and secure is all.

HOLMES. Move the light across the window, Jennie!

(WATSON takes the candle from BARRYMORE and does as directed.)

MRS. BARRYMORE. No, please, don't—

WATSON *(peering out the window)*. Ah, ha! See? Look there.

SIR HENRY & HOLMES. What?

SIR HENRY *(looks out the window)*. A tiny pinpoint of yellow light moving back and forth. It's a signal! Someone's out there. Is there a plot against me, Barrymore?

MRS. BARRYMORE. No, Sir Henry. It's all my doing. It is my younger brother, Selden.

SIR HENRY. Selden? He's the escaped convict?

BARRYMORE. He's all alone on the moor, sleeps in abandoned stone huts, Sir Henry. We bring him food. We can't let him starve to death.

SIR HENRY. He's a desperate man, Barrymore. Desperate men do desperate things in a desperate fashion.

HOLMES. Well phrased, Sir Henry.

SIR HENRY. We must capture him. The candle is less than a mile away. Get your revolver, Miss Watson.

BARRYMORE & MRS. BARRYMORE *(overlapping)*. Oh, please, no, you can't—

WATSON *(to AUDIENCE)*. I run to my bedroom and grab Uncle John's pistol. Then we're down the stairs and out the door and across the moor in the blink of an eye!

(LIGHTS down in Baskerville Hall and up on the moor. HOLMES is keenly watching the action.)

HOLMES. Careful, now, Jennie!

(EVERYONE steps cautiously as WATSON shares her thoughts and observations with the AUDIENCE and with HOLMES.

In the distance can be seen the brightening glow of SELDEN's signal candle.)

WATSON. A spectacular night! The moon bright in the sky with shadows everywhere and that misty moor stuff...so hard to see where we're going. But look... there in the distance...getting closer...the glow of Selden's candle!

(At this moment, MRS. BARRYMORE stumbles forward, almost losing her balance. BARRYMORE helps her regain her footing.)

SIR HENRY. Keep up, everyone! We're almost there.
ADLIBS *(from BARRYMORE and MRS. BARRYMORE)*. Don't hurt him, Sir Henry. He's my brother. Look out for that rock! I love him so.
WATSON. And then—

(SFX: A blood-curdling howl of gargantuan dimensions rolls back and forth across the moor! This is the Sound of The Hound as we've never heard it before!

ALL stop in their tracks, awash in a sense of impending doom.)

WATSON *(cont'd)*. It came with the wind through the silence of the night: a long, deep mutter, then a rising howl like a wounded beast.

HOLMES. At last! The Hound!

(As the Sound of The Hound fades away, DR. MORTIMER enters the action. She is out of breath.)

DR. MORTIMER. Is everyone all right? I was returning home from supper with the Stapletons when I—

SIR HENRY. I'm no coward, Miss Watson, but that sound froze my very blood. Is there truth to the legend, then?

WATSON. It's an old wives' tale, Sir—

DR. MORTIMER. What about that footprint of The Hound beside Sir Charles as he lay in the cold night air?

MRS. BARRYMORE *(stumbling forward into the darkness, desperately seeking signs of her brother)*. My brother's out here all alone. Selden!

(LIGHTS key on SELDEN in the distance, his face illuminated by the single candle.)

WATSON. Wait! Look! See? There in the distance!

(Poor SELDEN looks like a savage with his matted hair, bristling beard and small, cunning eyes.)

HOLMES. Oh, he doesn't look so good.

MRS. BARRYMORE *(yelling to SELDEN)*. Brother! We've come to help—

SIR HENRY. After him! Hurry! Don't let him get away!

(The chase is on, again in slow motion. SELDEN evades his pursuers.

SFX: Toss in the howling wind, the swirling mist, and all the rest of it…whatever can be thrown into the chase.)

ADLIBS. Watch out! Hurry! Run, Selden! Ow, my foot.

WATSON *(to AUDIENCE and HOLMES)*. Then comes the rain…and the mist…and Selden keeps getting further and further away…we'll never catch him… I pull out my revolver… *(WATSON does so)* …and take aim.

(MUSIC: Really tense stuff!

EVERYONE stops suddenly and looks at WATSON.)

MRS. BARRYMORE. No, please. He's my brother!

(It appears WATSON will shoot poor SELDEN. But after a moment, she lowers her revolver.)

WATSON *(to AUDIENCE)*. What was I thinking!? I couldn't bring myself to kill an unarmed man who so desperately wanted to live.

MRS. BARRYMORE. Thank you, Miss Watson. You have a generous heart.

HOLMES. The sporting thing to do, Jennie. Well done.

MRS. BARRYMORE. Thank you, thank you.

HOLMES. Catch him with your wits, my girl. Put your mind to it.

(SFX: Thunder approaching.)

DR. MORTIMER. Another storm's on the way. We'll all catch our death of cold out here.

SIR HENRY. Enough for one evening. We'll look for Selden again in the morning. Can't get far in all this boggy marsh.

(As they prepare to return to Baskerville Hall...)

WATSON *(to HOLMES)*. Then, as we are about to return, I catch a glimpse of a figure in the far distance.

(LIGHTS reveal the silhouette of a figure in the distance, standing on a small hill, surveying the moor.)

WATSON *(cont'd)*. It wasn't Selden, of that I'm sure.

HOLMES. Stapleton, perhaps?

WATSON. Not that I could tell. This was a man in a long coat, his arms folded across his chest. I turned and shouted out to...Sir Henry?

SIR HENRY *(turning toward WATSON)*. Yes, what, Miss Watson?

WATSON *(pointing)*. A man! Standing on that hill. There! *(Beat.)* But when I looked back...the man was gone.

SIR HENRY. Just your imagination, Miss Watson.

BARRYMORE. We've all had a fright. A very long night.

SIR HENRY. Perhaps some hot tea, Barrymore? Dr. Mortimer? Care to join us?

DR. MORTIMER. That's very kind of you, Sir Henry.

BARRYMORE. Careful, everyone.

(The LIGHTS fade down on the moor as SIR HENRY, BARRYMORE, DR. MORTIMER and MRS. BARRYMORE exit to Baskerville Hall.

WATSON moves into a LIGHT POOL.)

WATSON *(to HOLMES)*. A long night, indeed. Rain. Lightning flashes. That man, Selden, running through the night.

HOLMES. And that figure on the hill? I think I know who it is.

WATSON. You do? Who is it?

HOLMES. Soon, Jennie, all will be revealed. A few more odds and ends to wrap up first. You're doing wonderfully. Be well. Be safe! *(LIGHTS out on HOLMES.)*

WATSON *(to AUDIENCE)*. There she goes again! Leaving me to flounder around in the muck with an escaped whack-job screaming across the moor. And The Hound? Where does it hide during the day? Where does it get its food? So many questions and not a single answer to any of them.

(We hear the angry voices of BARRYMORE, MRS. BARRYMORE and SIR HENRY. LIGHTS down on WATSON and up in the breakfast room.)

WATSON *(referring to the angry voices)*. Oh, no. Hear that? More trouble. Lucky me!

(WATSON enters the argument. MRS. BARRYMORE is still visibly shaken from the ordeal on the moor.)

DR. MORTIMER. Ah, Miss Watson. You've stepped into the thick of it now.

MRS. BARRYMORE. My poor brother wouldn't hurt a fly, Miss Watson. I know he wouldn't.

(LIGHTS key on SELDEN peering through the breakfast room window. Only MRS. BARRYMORE knows he is there. SELDEN listens to the conversation, agreeing or disagreeing as appropriate.)

SIR HENRY *(to BARRYMORE)*. There are lonely houses scattered over the moor. He's a convict. He could do anything.

MRS. BARRYMORE. He's a good boy at heart. A little slow in the head is all.

(SELDEN isn't sure if he likes the sound of that.)

BARRYMORE. Always wanted to be liked. Fell in with a bad crowd. Picked the wrong friends, that was his crime.

MRS. BARRYMORE. They framed him, they did. Told the police he did the robbing and hit the night watchman over the head. But he couldn't have. He's not smart enough. Can't read or write. Can barely count all his fingers and toes.

(SELDEN thinks about that for a moment, then begins counting his fingers.)

BARRYMORE. We go out every night, leave food and clothing near the candle. Say nothing to the police, Sir Henry, please. In a few days he'll be on his way to Australia. His cousins will care for him there.

SIR HENRY. Poor, frightened soul. Sounds like he's suffered enough. Your thoughts, Miss Watson?

WATSON. I agree. There's nothing to be gained by putting Selden back into prison. Let the man enjoy his freedom. *(To AUDIENCE.)* We had no authority to free this man, I know, but it's in the original novel and we had to put it in the play.

MRS. BARRYMORE. Oh, thank you, both. I promise Selden will cause you no more trouble. Cross my heart.

(MRS. BARRYMORE and SELDEN exchange a quick look and wave to each other before the LIGHTS go out on SELDEN.)

WATSON. OK. Hubba-hubba! One mystery solved. What's next?

BARRYMORE. You've been a gentleman to the core, Sir Henry. I should like to do the best I can for you in return. I know why Sir Charles was at the gate so late that night.

WATSON. You do?

BARRYMORE. It was to meet a woman.

SIR HENRY. A woman? What woman?

BARRYMORE. We can't give you her name, but we can give you her initials.

SIR HENRY. Her initials?

(LIGHTS up in Sir Charles' study. A desk and chair, a fireplace or stove of some sort.

SIR CHARLES is looking out the study window.

ALL watch the proceedings that follow. Another "movie" is beginning.)

BARRYMORE *(as he enters the study, holding a sealed envelope).* Your uncle received a letter the morning he died. *(He hands the letter to SIR CHARLES.)*

SIR CHARLES. Thank you, Barrymore.

BARRYMORE. You're welcome, Sir Charles. *(To WATSON and the others.)* He lingered for a moment then opened the letter. As he began reading, he turned his back to me.

SIR CHARLES. That will be all, Barrymore.

(BARRYMORE bows and moves to the door. But then he stops, turns, and looks for a moment at SIR CHARLES.)

BARRYMORE. It was from a small village over the moor a few miles.

MRS. BARRYMORE. Addressed in a woman's hand.

WATSON *(to AUDIENCE).* A sense of mystery hung in the air.

BARRYMORE. I shouldn't have lingered I know, but Sir Charles seemed troubled by the letter's contents. I tried to catch a word or two.

(SIR CHARLES begins to read the letter aloud. His eye-sight is failing him. He mumbles.)

SIR CHARLES. My Dear Sir Charles… It is my sincere… hope…that…um…uh…blap…you might…zoop…

(From everywhere, once again, faces peer around set pieces and heads pop out of sound booths! All straining to hear a single word SIR CHARLES utters. As many as possible approach SIR CHARLES in an effort to hear what he is reading. Closer and closer. Some might even penetrate the scene.)

BARRYMORE. But the poor man began to mumble…and it was…I couldn't…hear what he…was…
SIR CHARLES. If…wurr…fortunate tha…um…um… dort…ah…desper…
EVERYONE ADLIBS *(in their effort to hear SIR CHARLES)*. What did he say? Can't hear a word he— Speak up, old man! That wasn't a nice thing to say!
BARRYMORE. Then suddenly he bent over and threw the letter into the fireplace. The letter went up in flames!

(EVERYONE gasps as SIR CHARLES tosses the letter into the flames. Then, while grumbling their disappoint-ment, EVERYONE returns to whatever they were doing prior to their arrival on the scene.)

EVERYONE ADLIBS *(to cover EVERYONE's exit, as needed)*. What'd he do that for? Couldn't hear a thing! Sounded like he was crunching popcorn! Came all the way out here for nothing!

WATSON. How unfortunate. Up in flames.

(SIR CHARLES seems deeply disturbed. He moves to the window and looks out.)

MRS. BARRYMORE. But then last week I went to his study to tidy up in preparation for your arrival.

(MRS. BARRYMORE enters the study and crosses to the fireplace. SIR CHARLES turns and watches the "movie" with considerable interest. MRS. BARRYMORE kneels down, cleans a bit, then notices the letter.)

MRS. BARRYMORE. I did my usual. A dusty over here, a dusty over there. Not necessary, really. He was such a neat, tidy man. Then, as I was scooping up the ashes in the back of the fireplace, I discovered the letter.

SIR CHARLES. Good for you, Mrs. Barrymore. Always so thorough. Tedious, but thorough.

MRS. BARRYMORE. It was mostly charred, Sir Henry.

DR. MORTIMER. Rotten luck, indeed.

MRS. BARRYMORE. But one little slip of paper, Sir Henry, the end of a page, you see…I could barely make out the—

DR. MORTIMER, SIR HENRY & WATSON *(with great impatience)*. Yes?

MRS. BARRYMORE. There…at the very bottom…if you looked very closely was—

DR. MORTIMER, SIR HENRY, WATSON & SIR CHARLES. Get on with it, woman!

MRS. BARRYMORE *(as if reading the letter)*. "Please, please, as you are a gentleman, burn this letter, and be at the gate by ten o'clock."

SIR CHARLES. Finally! Thank you. I thought you'd never get to it. But I do miss you. *(SIR CHARLES kisses MRS. BARRYMORE on the forehead.)*

(MRS. BARRYMORE touches her forehead absentmindedly. SIR CHARLES exits.

LIGHTS out in the study as MRS. BARRYMORE returns to the group.)

SIR HENRY. So, who signed the letter?

MRS. BARRYMORE. Oh, no signature, Sir Henry. Just the initials L.L.

SIR HENRY & WATSON. L.L.?

BARRYMORE. We didn't want to tell you before.

MRS. BARRYMORE. An older man with a younger woman. You know how people like to gossip.

SIR HENRY. I do understand but we've lost valuable time. L.L., eh? Tomorrow we need to find out to whom the initials L.L belong.

DR. MORTIMER. Laura Lyons. Lives two hills over. Being the only doctor around, you get to know the neighborhood. She had a bad sinus drip last month, in fact. Hope she's recovered.

WATSON. OK. Progress! Laura Lyons it is. I'll talk with her first thing tomorrow.

SIR HENRY. Yes, well, enough for tonight, everyone. I'm bushed. More in the morning.

(General "good nights" all around as ALL exit except WATSON. As the LIGHTS fade out on Baskerville Hall, WATSON steps into a LIGHT POOL.)

WATSON *(to AUDIENCE)*. I hardly slept a wink that night. Kept seeing poor Selden leaping from rock to rock with that crazed look in his eyes. And not to be able to count your fingers and toes! How dreadful is that! I counted mine all night. They're still there. So! After a quick cup of tea the next morning, I set out to interview Miss Laura Lyons.

SCENE 3 – LAURA SPILLS THE BEANS…ALMOST

(LIGHTS out on WATSON and up in Laura Lyons' parlor as WATSON moves into the scene.

A BANNER/SIGN appears with "Laura Lyons Spills the Beans…Almost" scrolled across it.)

WATSON *(to AUDIENCE)*. When I reached the residence, I was ushered into the parlor by a very eager looking maid. *(The MAID ushers WATSON into the room.)* Thank you.

MAID. Thank you? Is that all? Just thank you? Just nod my head and get off the stage? I have lines here! About the weather. And if I've heard some large dog barking! I'm ready! Give me the cue!

WATSON. We had to cut your lines. Sorry.

MAID. Sorry? What do you mean by sorry? I've been waiting over an hour for—

WATSON. We're running late.
MAID. Oh, man…what a bummer!

(The MAID begins to cry. Loudly. And exits in a huff.

LAURA LYONS enters.)

MISS LYONS. What did you say to that poor girl?
WATSON. Not now, Miss Lyons, I haven't much time. I'm Jennie Watson and I'm here to investigate the unfortunate death of Sir Charles. And I'd like to ask—

(LIGHTS key on SIR CHARLES as he listens in on the scene. Only WATSON can see and converse with him.)

WATSON *(to SIR CHARLES)*. What are you doing here?
SIR CHARLES. Just curious. I heard my name mentioned.
MISS LYONS. I live here! That's what I'm doing here. You came to see me, remember?
WATSON *(trying to keep these multiple realities clearly in mind)*. I did, yes. Uh…right…sorry! OK! I've learned you knew Sir Charles. Am I correct?
MISS LYONS. I owe a great deal to his kindness, yes. He assisted me through a difficult situation. What business is it of yours?
SIR CHARLES. That was nice of her to say, wasn't it?
WATSON *(trying to stay focused)*. What precisely was that difficult situation, Miss Lyons? Hunting for a wealthy husband, perhaps?
SIR CHARLES. Hey, now, Miss Watson.
MISS LYONS. How dare you?

WATSON. I dare a great deal. We regard this case as one of murder.

SIR CHARLES. I was murdered? Oh, goody! Push on then.

WATSON. Did you ever write Sir Charles asking him to meet you?

MISS LYONS. Certainly not. Why would I—?

SIR CHARLES. Laura?

HOLMES. "Please, please, as you are a gentleman, burn this letter, and be at the gate by ten o'clock"? Sound familiar?

MISS LYONS. Is there no such thing as a gentleman left in the world anymore? I asked Sir Charles to burn the letter after he—

SIR CHARLES. I did burn the letter but—

WATSON. The flames went out before it was all consumed, unfortunately.

MISS LYONS (the truth at last). Yes, I did write it. I was so desperate!

SIR CHARLES. Her husband gambled away all their money. I helped Laura survive on her own.

MISS LYONS. My husband wouldn't give me a divorce unless I could give him a huge sum of money to pay off his gambling debts. I hoped that an interview with Sir Charles might… He was such a generous man.

SIR CHARLES. I wish she hadn't used the past tense.

WATSON. But you never arrived that night. Something or someone stopped you, didn't something or someone?

MISS. LYONS. It is none of your business. It's my life.

SIR CHARLES (with a sense of longing). Too bad for me it wasn't you at the gate, my dear.

MISS LYONS. I refuse to answer any more of your questions, Miss Watson. My life is none of your business! Please leave this instant.

(The MAID enters.)

MAID. That goes for me, too! I had lines, lots of lines. I want my lines back!

(LIGHTS out on SIR CHARLES and in Laura Lyons' parlor as WATSON steps into a LIGHT POOL.)

WATSON *(to AUDIENCE)*. Not my best work, but I can tell Miss Lyons is hiding something. Got all fidgety and wouldn't look me in the eye. The next two days and nights passed without incident. Sir Henry kept poring over Sir Charles' papers and I kept walking the moor trying to find where The Hound was. Got lost twice! Stapleton had to rescue me.

(LIGHTS key on STAPLETON.)

STAPLETON. I've warned you, Miss Watson. The moor is no place for a city girl. I may not be around to save you next time. *(LIGHTS out quickly on STAPLETON.)*

WATSON *(to AUDIENCE)*. Such a spooky man. I felt so foolish. But I couldn't drop the ball now! Too much at stake. Then…last night I just had to clear my mind…

SCENE 4 – DEATH ON THE MOOR COMING UP SOON

(A BANNER/SIGN appears with "Death on the Moor Coming Up Soon" scrolled across it.)

WATSON *(cont'd., to AUDIENCE)*. I entered the garden where poor Sir Charles had died. There was no wind. So still. Unnerving. As if the moor were holding its breath. And then...yes, see? Look! The moon broke through the clouds and...there, on the small hill beyond the garden gate stood the figure I'd seen on the moor. It looked vaguely familiar but I had to find out for sure. I opened the gate and moved forward across the moor.

(LIGHTS fade down as WATSON begins sneaking up on the figure. WATSON and the figure are barely visible.

MUSIC: Appropriate "sneaking-up" music.)

WATSON *(cont'd)*. Slowly...closer...closer... *(slowly extending her hand)* and as I was about to reach out... and grab the figure...

(LIGHTS key on HOLMES as she spins around swiftly and strikes a "how do I look" pose. She is dressed out in long pants, shirt, long coat, and maybe even a deerstalker cap. Hair tucked inside the cap; or perhaps she is in a ponytail and the tail hangs down behind her. She is holding a flamboyant meerschaum pipe so often associated with Sherlock Holmes.)

HOLMES. Jennie! You found me at last. Well done, girl.

WATSON. Shirley?

HOLMES. You said you wanted my help. Here I am. What do you think?

WATSON. Well, it's not Halloween, you know?

HOLMES. Uncle Sherlock does his best thinking in this getup, so I thought I'd give it a shot.

WATSON. Have you been here all along?

HOLMES. Here, there, snooping everywhere. Couldn't let the villain think two great minds were at work at the same time, eh? Scare him away for sure. I took a room three towns over. A lovely little place. The Chez Marriott. I highly recommend it.

WATSON. And how did you know I was sneaking up on you?

HOLMES *(as only a close friend can reveal)*. Your perfume, my dear. You always put on way too much. I knew you were coming from a mile away. We'll talk about that later. But now we must—

(SFX: A prolonged human scream of horror and anguish engulfs the moor.)

HOLMES *(cont'd)*. Oh, no! Are we too late? It came from over there. Hurry, Jennie!

(HOLMES and WATSON run in place as WATSON speaks to the AUDIENCE.

Both respond to the conditions WATSON describes.)

WATSON. We began running blindly toward the scream, losing our footing in the darkness, blundering against boulders.

HOLMES. Watch on your right, Jennie!

(SFX: The same tormented scream as before only much closer than before.

MUSIC: Suspense on the moor stuff!)

WATSON. Again the agonized cry swept through the silent night, louder now and much nearer than before. But then a new sound...louder still...so very frightening!!

(SFX: Now a deep, labored panting of an animal can be heard. Could it be The Hound? Closer and closer. A blending of terrifying human and inhuman sounds and then a "Nooooo!!!" followed by a dull, heavy thud!

HOLMES and WATSON come to a halt. They are winded but still on their feet.)

WATSON. We halted...and listened. Not another...sound broke the silence of the...windless...night.

HOLMES. The Hound has beaten us, Jennie. We are too late.

(LIGHTS key on a fallen body, face down, wearing the same overcoat SIR HENRY wore in the opening scene at 221B Baker Street. HOLMES and WATSON approach cautiously.)

WATSON. Oh, no. It's Sir Henry!

HOLMES. Yes. I recognize the coat he wore when we first met in London. Poor man! *(HOLMES kneels down to get a better look at the body, peeking at the face.)*

WATSON. It's all my fault! I should have been more—

HOLMES *(overlapping)*. Wait, Jennie! This man has a beard!

WATSON. A beard? It must be the convict, Selden. Sir Henry is still alive!

HOLMES. Give me a hand, Jennie.

(WATSON helps HOLMES turn over the body as STAPLETON arrives from one direction and DR. MORTIMER from another.

DR. MORTIMER holds a doctor's medical bag in one hand and a raised lantern in the other.)

STAPLETON. I heard screams. Dreadful cries.

DR. MORTIMER *(overlapping)*. Is everyone all right? I heard—

STAPLETON *(having some difficulty seeing)*. Who's that on the ground? Not Sir Henry, I hope.

WATSON. It's Selden. The escaped convict.

DR. MORTIMER *(moving to the body)*. Here, let me have a look.

STAPLETON *(startled for a moment)*. Selden? But he's wearing Sir Henry's coat. *(Revealing SIR HENRY's scarf.)* And I found Sir Henry's scarf on the path just now.

WATSON. I suspect Sir Henry gave them to Barrymore. To keep Selden warm on the moor.

DR. MORTIMER. There are no marks that I can find.

STAPLETON. Who is that with you, Dr. Mortimer? I don't recognize—

HOLMES *(approaching STAPLETON)*. Shirley Holmes at your service, sir.

STAPLETON. You're Sherlock Holmes' niece, correct?

HOLMES. I am indeed. Miss Watson and I heard a cry and came running.

DR. MORTIMER. As did I. I was returning from Sir Henry's with some estate papers he needed to sign before the morning postal train.

STAPLETON. I heard it too. I was worried about Sir Henry.

WATSON. Worried? For what reason?

STAPLETON. I had suggested he drop by this evening for a bit of supper. I was quite rude to him earlier last week and wanted to make it up to him. But he never arrived. And then…those…screams. I became alarmed for his safety.

HOLMES. His safety, why?

STAPLETON. Because of all the legends about the phantom hound that roams the moor. Isn't that why you're here, Miss Holmes? To protect Sir Henry from legends and superstitions?

HOLMES. I didn't hear any hound sounds, did you, Jennie?

WATSON. Hound sounds? Not a one, no. None. No hound sounds around here!

HOLMES. Anxiety and exposure disoriented Selden, I suspect, Mr. Stapleton. He ran himself off the cliff there most likely. Elementary deduction, really.

STAPLETON. Must be fascinating having a famous uncle for a detective. Please drop by for dinner tomorrow evening, won't you, and thrill me with all his elementary deductions? And Sir Henry as well, of course.

HOLMES. Very generous of you.

STAPLETON. Now, may I help you with Selden's body?

WATSON. No, we're fine. We carry dead bodies around all the time. Not a problem.

STAPLETON. As you wish. But remember! Lose your bearings, you'll end up like Selden. Oh, and Happy Halloween, Miss Holmes. *(STAPLETON hands the scarf to HOLMES then exits.)*

HOLMES *(to WATSON)*. We carry dead bodies around all the time? Where did that come from?

WATSON. I don't know! It just popped out.

DR. MORTIMER. Ladies, let's put poor Selden in my horse wagon and take him back to Baskerville Hall. Grab something. Ready?

(All three struggle with lifting SELDEN. They even try to drape him over WATSON's shoulders similar to a fireman's carry.)

HOLMES *(laboring with SELDEN)*. I don't think I like that man. His tone. Thrill me with all his elementary deductions!

WATSON. "Happy Halloween" wasn't very nice either.

(Suddenly, they all stumble and down goes SELDEN. Undaunted, they grab wrists and ankles as best they can and lift him partway off the ground, only to end up bumping him up and down along the path.)

ADLIBS *(overlapping)*. Pull. Good. More. Harder. Too hard. Oh, dear. That must have hurt. He's dead, I forgot. I have to go to the bathroom. Not now, Jennie. Almost there. Good. Oops! A little further.

(After a particularly hard "bump," SELDEN's eyes pop open. He reacts audibly, as well, to this painful mistreatment of the dead.)

SELDEN *(interspersed as needed)*. Watch that! Put me down! Ouch. You'll be the death of me! Someone help me!

(The women, of course, do not hear SELDEN's commentary and continue pulling until, thankfully, SELDEN is off the stage!)

SCENE 5 – BAITING THE TRAP

(LIGHTS down on the moor and up on Baskerville Hall as WATSON, DR. MORTIMER and HOLMES enter with SELDEN. The commotion brings BARRYMORE, MRS. BARRYMORE and SIR HENRY into the scene.

There is much confusion as everyone helps with SELDEN's body.)

WATSON. This is Shirley Holmes, everyone. She's helping with…watch it, his pants are falling off!

(MRS. BARRYMORE collapses into tears. Very loud tears! We might be in the middle of an Italian opera here! SELDEN continues with his protestations.)

ADLIBS *(overlapping)*. My poor brother, oh, no! That hurts! His pants, his pants! Watch his head! Don't drop him! Oh, you did, you dropped him!

(At last, DR. MORTIMER, BARRYMORE and MRS. BARRYMORE exit, dragging SELDEN's battered body behind them.)

SIR HENRY. We heard his screams. Poor man. I was about to leave but I'd promised you I wouldn't walk the moor at night. A coward's promise. I should have—
HOLMES. You did the right thing, Sir Henry. The Hound was after you.
SIR HENRY. Me?
WATSON. Selden was wearing your overcoat. *(Producing the scarf.)* And your scarf.

(The dialogue overlaps at breakneck speed. Time is of the essence!)

SIR HENRY. The one I gave to Barrymore—
WATSON. To give to Selden to keep him warm on the moor, yes.
SIR HENRY. So he died because of me.
HOLMES. No time for self-pity, Sir Henry. Stapleton has invited us to dinner tomorrow evening. You will accept.
SIR HENRY. I will?
HOLMES. Yes.

SIR HENRY. And you and Watson?

HOLMES. Tell him we had to return to London suddenly.

WATSON. We did? I mean we do?

HOLMES. Things to do, people to see. Have Perkins drive you over, but tell Stapleton that after dinner you'll be walking home across the moor.

SIR HENRY. But you said I shouldn't—

HOLMES. You must trust us, Sir Henry. It will be your finest hour.

WATSON. Spooky is as spooky does, Sir. Henry. You'll be safe with us.

SIR HENRY. Well, I don't like it, but I'll do as you ask.

HOLMES *(pulling WATSON off to one side)*. Spooky is as spooky does? Where did that come from?

WATSON *(whispering in reply)*. I don't know. I'm really stressed. There's a lot of weird stuff going down here!

HOLMES. Well, get a grip!

WATSON. OK, OK...I've got it now!

(DR. MORTIMER enters.)

DR. MORTIMER. We've put Selden in the study for now. I'll contact the authorities in the morning. They'll come for his body.

(MRS. BARRYMORE lunges into the room, sobbing, crying, her hands flailing helplessly in front of her. She lurches, stumbles and staggers offstage, wailing as she goes.

BARRYMORE enters after her.)

BARRYMORE. I've made up a room for you, Miss Holmes.

HOLMES. That's very gracious of—

(MRS. BARRYMORE wails offstage again. BARRY-MORE bows to SIR HENRY and then bolts after his wife.)

SIR HENRY. That's quite a sound she makes, isn't it? Enough to wake the dead!

DR. MORTIMER. She'll recover, she's a hardy soul. Well, I'm off. I'll be back tomorrow night, Sir Henry, with the last of the estate papers for you to sign. Sleep tight.

(As DR. MORTIMER exits, MRS. BARRYMORE again lurches into the scene, flailing even more, then exits sobbing even louder...if that's possible.

BARRYMORE, ever faithful, enters in pursuit, pauses ever so briefly to bow to SIR HENRY, beckons to HOLMES to follow him, then races after his wife.)

SIR HENRY. Yes, well, good night, all. Come on, Miss Holmes. *(SIR HENRY exits, followed by HOLMES.)*

HOLMES *(waving to WATSON as she exits)*. Wonderful work, Jennie. Get your sleep. Tomorrow's the big day! *(HOLMES is gone.)*

WATSON *(to AUDIENCE)*. What a night. Poor Selden's horrible screams. Then his lifeless body! And no teeth marks anywhere. Was there really a hound out on the moor? And what did Shirley have in mind for Sir Henry tomorrow night? I felt in the dark again. It's not easy being a detective, I'll tell you that. No sleep. No food. You start seeing things.

(Right on cue, MRS. BARRYMORE enters screaming and wailing. She staggers across stage and exits.

Then SELDEN appears! His palms are covering his ears in an effort to block out his sister's horrendous wailing. SELDEN is about to make his escape when BARRY-MORE enters, blocking SELDEN's exit.

Upon seeing each other, both SELDEN and BARRY-MORE scream. They do a "double take" to WATSON who shrugs, as if to say, "I can't believe this either!"

Thankfully for all concerned, MRS. BARRYMORE wails again offstage. BARRYMORE looks one last time at SELDEN to be sure he's seeing what he thinks he's seeing, smiles at WATSON...then exits in pursuit of his wailing wife.

Free at last, SELDEN looks at WATSON, smiles, waves goodbye and exits through the gates of Baskerville Hall and out across the moor. Or out a window. Or how about through the audience and out the doors at the back of the theater?

WATSON waves goodbye to SELDEN as he makes his departure.

Note: If the final exit of the MESSENGER was made through the theater, the MESSENGER could appear briefly, get SELDEN's attention and encourage him to follow the MESSENGER's example!)

WATSON *(cont'd., to AUDIENCE).* Did I see what I think I just saw? No…not possible. I need some sleep. What a night. See you in the morning.

(LIGHTS bump down quickly on WATSON.

MUSIC: Night falling quickly!

Then, almost instantly, the LIGHTS pop up brightly in the breakfast room. It is day! WATSON's LIGHT POOL pops up as well.

SFX and MUSIC: A great day a'comin'!)

WATSON *(cont'd., to AUDIENCE. Popping awake!).* Whoa! What a night. I must have fallen asleep standing straight up!

(HOLMES enters refreshed, eager, ready to go.)

HOLMES *(to WATSON).* Today's the big day.
WATSON. Shirley, is Selden still in the study, you think?
HOLMES. Of course he is. He can't just get up and run out the door, dear girl! He's dead!

(WATSON looks at the AUDIENCE as if to say, "She doesn't know what we know, eh?"

BARRYMORE enters with a cup of tea for WATSON.

LIGHTS out on WATSON as she moves into the break-fast room and takes the cup of tea from BARRYMORE.)

WATSON. Thank you, Barrymore. Is Mrs. Barrymore feel-ing any—

(As might be expected, the wailing sobs of MRS. BAR-RYMORE fill the breakfast room. WATSON almost drops her tea cup. BARRYMORE smiles sheepishly and continues to busy himself with the scones and jam.)

HOLMES *(in a hush-hush fashion)*. No time for pleasant-ries, Jennie. I must catch this morning's train to London. Hold down the fort here. Keep your eye on Sir Henry. And no sneaking across the moor.

WATSON *(whispering)*. Will do. But who do you think did it? Just a hint. Dr. Mortimer? She's the legal beagle type, right? Contracts and wills and all that. She could forge everything! With Sir Henry dead, she could have it all!

HOLMES. Patience, patience.

WATSON. And I know Barrymore makes a nice cup of tea and all, but he has that black beard; and if Sir Henry doesn't actually live here, then the Barrymores can have the whole place to themselves! And Mrs. Barrymore's tears? They seem a little much, don't you think?

(Again, right on cue, we hear MRS. BARRYMORE wail-ing away somewhere in Baskerville Hall.)

WATSON *(cont'd)*. Hear what I mean?

HOLMES. All will be revealed shortly, girlfriend. Never fear.

WATSON. You always say that and then you don't reveal zilch. I've doing all the heavy lifting out here. All you do is play dress-up on the moor!

HOLMES. Play dress-up on the moor? Oh, well done. Just wait 'til I tell you about your perfume!

WATSON. What? Tell me what about my perfume?

HOLMES. Tonight at nine o'clock, Jennie. Meet me at the Stapleton house. Don't be late. Don't wear that perfume. Bye for now. *Ciao*, Barrymore.

WATSON *(pursuing HOLMES)*. What about my perfume? Don't leave me here again!

(HOLMES is gone again.

LIGHTS down on Baskerville Hall as WATSON steps into a LIGHT POOL.)

WATSON *(to AUDIENCE)*. What's with all that "*Ciao*, Barrymore!" stuff? And what's she going to say about my perfume? I spent most of the day sulking and waiting for nine o'clock to come around. Sir Henry buried his nose in Sir Charles' financial ledgers, and the Barrymores kept searching high and low for Selden's body. They were looking in old attic trunks the last time I checked. Then, finally…

(LIGHTS change instantly, with authority!)

WATSON *(cont'd)*. Bam! Night fell. Just like that. Dark and cold it was. A stiff wind howling. *(SFX)* Something awful was going to happen. But thrilling, too. I couldn't wait!

SCENE 6 – THE HOUND AT LAST

(LIGHTS key on the outside of the STAPLETON dining room. A dining room window partially covered by curtains is featured prominently.

A SIGN/BANNER appears with "The Hound at Last" scrolled across it.

The night is dark but the moon is bright when it can be. Shadows abound where they should.

LIGHTS down on WATSON as she moves into the scene.)

WATSON *(to AUDIENCE)*. When I arrived I stayed back in the shadows. Tried to get my bearings. Then…
HOLMES. Psst! Jennie? Over here.
WATSON. Shirley? Is that you?

(LIGHTS key on HOLMES and LESTRADE. WATSON joins them.)

HOLMES. Yes. Ssh! Hi. *(Making introductions.)* Victoria, my comrade, Jennie Watson.
LESTRADE *(shaking WATSON's hand vigorously)*. Victoria Lestrade. A pleasure. I'm filling in for dear, old Dad who's got the flu. Lucky me!

HOLMES. Uncle Sherlock uses the Lestrade Dectective Agency all the time when he needs backup. Pulled her out of philosophy class this morning.

LESTRADE *(a bit overeager. Quite a bit, actually)*. I'm ready. Can't wait, can't wait! What's the plan? What do I do? Let's hop to it.

HOLMES. Down, girl! Easy. Do as I say and we'll catch ourselves a dastardly devil. Ready, everyone?

LESTRADE & WATSON. Ready!

(LIGHTS shift as WATSON, LESTRADE and HOLMES approach the house.)

WATSON *(to AUDIENCE)*. I could feel the tension increase as we approached the Stapleton house. Was Sir Henry safe? Was he dead already?

HOLMES. Jennie, peek into the window. See what you can see.

WATSON *(to AUDIENCE as she gets closer to the house)*. My heart is pounding. I inch my way up the side of the house until I can peek in through a window.

HOLMES. What do you see?

WATSON. Stapleton, Sir Henry and Miss Stapleton. They've finished dinner. Stapleton is gesturing. Now he's laughing. Now he's…wait! He's on his feet…he's leaving the room…

STAPLETON *(offstage)*. I'll be right back. I forgot to lock the barn door.

(A moment later, STAPLETON appears. He carries a parcel. He walks across the stage and exits.

MUSIC: Each step underscored by an eerie note or two.

After STAPLETON exits, WATSON follows a short distance and observes STAPLETON.)

WATSON *(whispering to HOLMES)*. It's a small…barn. He's taking out a key. Opening the door. Wait! I hear something…

LESTRADE. What do you hear?

WATSON. It's like a…growling sound, maybe? I'm not certain.

LESTRADE. A growling sound? What do you mean by growling? *(To HOLMES.)* I don't like growling sounds.

WATSON. Wait…he's coming back!

(STAPLETON suddenly appears. He is not carrying the parcel. He walks past WATSON who lets out a strange sound. Like a squeak. A gulp. Something that catches STAPLETON's attention.

STAPLETON pauses, turns, cocks his head as he tries to place the sound. WATSON is pressed flat as she can get against the wall of the house. About a foot away from STAPLETON.

MUSIC: Tension! Tension!)

WATSON *(to AUDIENCE)*. He had linguine with clam sauce. Glad I didn't wear my perfume.

(Then laughter from the dining room.

STAPLETON turns and reenters the house.

WATSON returns to HOLMES and LESTRADE.)

HOLMES. Well done, Jennie.

LESTRADE. Ditto for me!

WATSON *(pointing out over the heads of the AUDI-ENCE).* Yes, but look at that! *(To AUDIENCE.)* A dense fog was fast approaching. A white, woolly-looking, creeping thing that swallowed up half the moor. It curled itself around the corners of the house and rolled slowly up the walls.

(As the fog engulfs the stage, the Stapleton house disappears. All that barely can be seen now are WATSON, HOLMES and LESTRADE.

LIGHTS and a fog machine will do nicely here. The more fog the better!

Note: See Production Notes for alternative staging options.

MUSIC: Creeping fog stuff!)

LESTRADE. This is creepy stuff, Holmes. Can't even see the house anymore!

HOLMES. Sir Henry has got to leave soon or we'll lose him in the fog. We have to move back. To higher ground. Hurry.

(HOLMES, LESTRADE and WATSON seek higher ground as best they can.

It is almost impossible to see clearly. The fog is playing havoc with the moonlight. Jagged rocks and shrubs all conspire to create the most eerie and threatening shapes.

SFX and MUSIC can have a field day here.

Then...from the distance is heard...the sound of running feet! Someone gasping for breath!)

HOLMES *(cont'd)*. Get ready!

LESTRADE. Ready for what? Was this part of the deal? I don't think I like this!

(The sounds get closer and louder. And now we can hear the growling of a beast as well as the panting of a man running for his life!

Suddenly SIR HENRY bursts through the fog. He looks frightened beyond all comprehension. He grabs his chest, stumbles, loses his balance...falls to the ground.)

WATSON. Sir Henry!

(Just as WATSON begins to move to SIR HENRY, the blood-curdling Sound of The Hound echoes across the moor!

And out of the fog leaps the dreaded Hound! It's mouth agape, its eyes aflame. A terrible beast to behold. And he's charging right at SIR HENRY!

Note: What happens next is determined by the resources and artistic ingenuity of the production staff. As a reference, the following description of The Hound has been excerpted from the original story:

"A hound it was, an enormous coal-black hound, but not such a hound as mortal eyes have ever seen. Fire burst from its open mouth, its eyes glowed with a smouldering glare, its muzzle and hackles and dewlap *[the loose, hanging fold of skin on an animal's neck]* were outlined in flickering flame. Never in the delirious dream of a disordered brain could anything more savage, more appalling, more hellish, be conceived than that dark form and savage face which broke upon us out of the wall of fog."

Effective LIGHTING underscored by MUSIC, SFX and imaginative fog effects, should go far in giving the audience the jolt it has been anticipating. And while this play is presented as a comic thriller, the emphasis at this particular moment should be placed more on the thrilling than on the comedic.

Now, to pick up the action, all of which moves at break-neck speed!)

HOLMES. Watson. The revolver! Hurry!

(In a matter of seconds...

WATSON fumbles with the revolver, finally aims it and fires. The bullet misses!

SIR HENRY stumbles, loses his footing.

HOLMES, in a moment of insane bravery, screams and charges The Hound, grabbing and pulling whatever she can get hold of.

WATSON tries to fire again, but her revolver jams! Then she, too, attacks the beast with all the strength she has.)

ADLIBS *(interspersed as needed).* Look out! Stop! Don't! Help! I can't—! I'll get it! Shoot it! Oh, no, oh, no! It's jammed! Help me! I can't breathe!! I can't hold it! It's—

(LESTRADE draws her weapon and fires off three shots. One of the bullets may have hit its target.

Suddenly The Hound leaps into the fog and disappears. LESTRADE fires after it.

SFX: Underscoring the above are as many screeches and screams and howls and thunderclaps as can be compressed and amplified in ten seconds at the very most.

The Sound of The Hound reverberates across the moor!

Then...at last...all is quiet except for a groan or two. Even the fog seems to be catching its breath!)

ADLIBS *(as needed).* Anybody hurt? My arm, I think. My back. What happened? So much to—! My head hurts. Sir Henry? Over here. Is it gone? Be careful!

(Ah, moonbeams at last!

LIGHTS key on SIR HENRY who is regaining his strength. LESTRADE stands guard. WATSON and HOLMES look exhausted, but exhilarated. WATSON has been slightly wounded. The dialogue overlaps.)

HOLMES. Did you shoot it, Victoria?
LESTRADE. I'm not sure. So hard to see. May have.
WATSON. Sir Henry?
SIR HENRY. I am fine. Jennie, you?
WATSON. My arm, I think, is... *(Holding up her hand. Her fingers seem to glow in the dark.)* Look! Phosphorous, I suspect. Painted all over its face, around its eyes. Intended to flare in the moonlight.
SIR HENRY. Absolutely terrifying. You all saved my life.
HOLMES. Only after putting it in grave danger. I didn't count on the fog.
WATSON. Or my revolver jamming. So very sorry, Sir Henry.
SIR HENRY. Nothing risked, nothing gained, ladies. A wonderful adventure!

(WATSON falls to one knee.)

HOLMES. Jennie!

LESTRADE. I think she might be—

HOLMES. Jennie, are you—?

(HOLMES moves quickly to WATSON as BARRYMORE arrives with a pitchfork at the ready, followed closely by DR. MORTIMER who brandishes a knife or a threatening medical implement of some sort.)

HOLMES. Ah, Dr. Mortimer. Jennie's been—

(DR. MORTIMER moves to WATSON and examines the wound.)

BARRYMORE *(overlapping).* Sir Henry, are you—?

SIR HENRY. Fine, Barrymore, thank you.

BARRYMORE. We heard the horrible howling. Are we safe? Did you kill it?

HOLMES. Victoria got off a good shot or two, may have wounded the beast.

SIR HENRY. Then it leaped through the fog and disappeared. A gargantuan bloodhound with a head as big as a—

DR. MORTIMER. Quickly! Watson's arm...several bad scratches here. Need to wash these wounds. Get her back to Baskerville Hall. I can assist her better there.

WATSON *(a bit lightheaded).* Don't worry about me... I'm...fine...

(BARRYMORE and SIR HENRY help WATSON to her feet.)

SIR HENRY. And what about that coward Stapleton?

HOLMES. He must have heard us fighting for our lives. He's out there somewhere, lurking.

LESTRADE. After him anytime you're ready, Shirley, I am, I am!

HOLMES. For the moment, we'll get Jennie cleaned up. Then we'll go after Stapleton. Ready, everyone?

(EVERYONE begins to exit as the LIGHTS fade down on the moor and up on Baskerville Hall.)

SCENE 7 – SHIRLEY WRAPS IT ALL UP FOR US

(A BANNER/SIGN appears with "Shirley Wraps It All Up for Us" scrolled across it.

As WATSON is being transported to Baskerville Hall, she addresses the AUDIENCE.)

WATSON *(to AUDIENCE)*. What a night! Missed my first shot. Hand was shaking like an earthquake. Then my revolver jammed. But did you see Shirley? She was magnificent. And then I...I can't believe I really did it...I jumped on that thing myself...with...my...bare hands? I couldn't live with myself if I let that beast eat Shirley for dinner.

(BARRYMORE has alerted MRS. BARRYMORE who has prepared towels, bandages, soap, a basin of warm water.

DR. MORTIMER attends to WATSON's wounds while BARRYMORE and MRS. BARRYMORE serve food and hot tea. There is a general hubbub with overlapping commentary as everyone regains their equilibrium.)

LESTRADE *(reaching for the food with considerable gusto)*. A dreadful night. But great fun, eh, Shirley.
DR. MORTIMER. What a beast!
LESTRADE. Its breath smelled like stale enchiladas.
SIR HENRY. So, it was Stapleton all along. The phony beard, the threatening letter. What a nasty fellow he is.

(Suddenly STAPLETON and MISS STAPLETON appear in the doorway. STAPLETON looks crazed, like a man possessed. And he's holding a revolver.

MISS STAPLETON looks exhausted, frightened; she hangs back in the half darkness.)

STAPLETON. Yes, it was I all along! And I have been a little nasty, I admit.

(There is general confusion at STAPLETON's entrance. BARRYMORE shields MRS. BARRYMORE.)

LESTRADE *(getting set for action)*. He has a gun!
HOLMES. Easy, everyone. Put down the revolver, Mr. Stapleton. You don't want to hurt anybody.
STAPLETON. Oh, but I do! Very much!
MISS STAPLETON. I tried to make him listen to reason but he wouldn't stop. He's ill. He needs special help.

(LAURA LYONS bursts into the room. It is clear she has been running a considerable distance.)

HOLMES. Miss Lyons.

MISS LYONS.. I was so worried about… And then the… shots…on…the…moor. And the terrible howling… I just had to see if… *(To STAPLETON.)* John, darling, are you all right?

MISS STAPLETON *(to STAPLETON)*. Why is this woman calling you "John, Darling," John?

MISS LYONS. Your brother has proposed to me, Miss Stapleton. And I have accepted.

MISS STAPLETON. Proposed? My brother? Well, you can just un-accept his proposal. John Darling is not my brother. He's my husband!

LESTRADE. It just gets better and better.

STAPLETON. I want what is mine. The money. The land. Everything that is mine. I did what I had to do!

SIR HENRY. I am the last of the Baskervilles, you nut case!

HOLMES. Not really, Sir Henry.

SIR HENRY. What's that?

HOLMES. You both are Hugo's descendants.

ALL. Is that so?

(HOLMES points at the portrait of Sir Hugo Baskerville hanging prominently on the wall.)

HOLMES. There! Don't you see the resemblance? The forehead? The brow?

BARRYMORE. Wait! I think… Someone give me a hand with—

(BARRYMORE takes the portrait down from the wall and holds it next to STAPLETON's face so a comparison can be made.

STAPLETON is thrown off his game, uncertain where to point the revolver but eager to be sure everyone sees the similarities.)

HOLMES. See? If you cover up Hugo's beard and all that hair on top... *(HOLMES places her hands over Sir Hugo's beard and hair.)*

WATSON. And squint your eyes real tight...you can see... the...

(MRS. BARRYMORE and SIR HENRY move to the portrait.)

MRS. BARRYMORE. Those same thin, sneering lips, yes!

SIR HENRY. And those cold, intolerant eyes.

(STAPLETON preens a bit, turning his profile this way and that to insure the resemblance is made.)

LESTRADE *(overlapping)*. Shirley? The light's better over here.

HOLMES. Excellent. Step into the light, won't you, Mr. Stapleton?

(STAPLETON moves to the better light, unaware a trap is being set for him. But MISS STAPLETON sees what is about to happen.)

MISS STAPLETON. John, watch out for—

(LESTRADE and SIR HENRY grapple with STAPLETON and disarm him.)

MISS STAPLETON *(overlapping)*. Oh, no, no, don't hurt him, please!
MISS LYONS. Oh, yes, yes, hurt him all you want! He's lied to me!
SIR HENRY. This is madness. Does anybody know what's going on?
HOLMES. Actually, I do. Here comes the wrap-up! Everybody ready?

(At this point, EVERYONE INVOLVED WITH THE PRODUCTION makes an appearance. In period costume or contemporary street clothes. Technicians, London street people, henchmen, light-board operators, assistant directors, Sir Charles, even Selden. The more the merrier! They listen to the revelations and explanations and comment as indicated.

EVERYONE sees everyone else from this point on.)

EVERYONE. Ready!

(SFX: Drum roll or fanfare.)

HOLMES. While Jennie was here at Baskerville Hall…
WATSON. Slogging through the Murky Moor all by myself!
HOLMES. Jennie!

WATSON. Sorry.

HOLMES. I knew if we both arrived here that the villain would never show his face. So I went to the British Museum instead. Day after day. I examined old letters. Business records. Passenger ship records. Everything. And Eureka! *(To STAPLETON.)* Your real name is not John Stapleton.

EVERYONE. It's not?

HOLMES. It's Rodger Baskerville, the abandoned son of poor Sir Charles' younger brother.

EVERYONE *(said in unison or divided among groups).* You mean the sinister, dark, twisted younger brother who fled to South America and was mentioned briefly by Dr. Mortimer at the beginning of the play? But so long ago that the audience has completely forgotten?

HOLMES. The very same. Who grew up in Costa Rica, married Miss Stapleton and was hired in northern England as a schoolmaster to teach entomology.

EVERYONE *(in unison).* Entomology! Eeew! Bugs! We know that one!

HOLMES. But there's more!

EVERYONE *(in unison).* We can't wait!

HOLMES. So I took the train to northern England and discovered that the very same school had been robbed of all its money three years ago.

EVERYONE. No!

HOLMES. Yes! And that the very next day, Professor Buggy here and his wife mysteriously disappeared. I put two and five together—

LESTRADE. Seven!

HOLMES *(giving LESTRADE a "thumbs up" without skipping a beat).* And ten days later they bought the little cottage next door to Baskerville Hall to see what they could see.

SIR CHARLES *(looking angrily at STAPLETON)*. And they saw me. Rolling in money! You little pipsqueak!

STAPLETON *(to SIR CHARLES)*. You were old and frail. Had a bad heart. All I had to do was to get you—

MISS STAPLETON *(to SIR CHARLES)*. To fall in love with me, Sir Charles. So I could lure you into the moor where that awful dog would...

HOLMES. But Miss Stapleton refused to help her obsessed husband.

SIR CHARLES. Thank you, my dear.

MISS LYONS. So he found me!

EVERYONE *(in unison)*. Oh, oh!

MISS LYONS *(slaps STAPLETON)*. He looked so kind. *(Slaps STAPLETON.)* So gentle. *(Slaps STAPLETON again.)* So understanding. *(Slaps STAPLETON a fourth time. STAPLETON sags considerably.)* I told him about my husband's debts and he suggested I write you a letter, Sir Charles, seeking your assistance.

SIR CHARLES *(a bit spacy)*. Ah, yes, the letter. I remember. Right, Barrymore?

BARRYMORE. Absolutely, sir. Fine memory for a dead man.

SIR CHARLES *(to MISS LYONS)*. Go on, young lady. I can barely stand up here.

MISS LYONS *(to MISS STAPLETON)*. But after I sent the letter, John appeared at my door and said he should be the one to help me instead of Sir Charles. That he wanted to marry me and care for me the rest of our lives. That's why I did not show up at the gate that night, Sir Charles.

HOLMES. But Mr. Stapleton did show up at the gate, didn't you, Mr. Stapleton?

STAPLETON. Yes, I did! I did!

WATSON. You and that poor animal you've tortured.

STAPLETON. Get him, boy! Over the fence you go, [you devil hound!] Get him! Get him!

(SFX: The Sound of The Hound.

Hearing his cue, SIR CHARLES clutches his chest once more.)

SIR CHARLES. That's my cue!

(Fear again enters his eyes. He begins running in place as we saw at the beginning of the play. And, of course, he dies once again. This time, however, he might die on the stairs, or across a table, or hanging onto someone's shirt before sliding to the ground.

EVERYONE, as appropriate, applauds SIR CHARLES' rather ham-handed death scene.)

ADLIBS *(as needed)*. That looked really good, Sir Charles Nice job! Sweet work. Love that eye thing you do at the last. Great shoulders.

SIR CHARLES *(coming alive once again)*. Thank you, thank you. Well, good show, everyone. See you all at curtain call. *(SIR CHARLES waves to the AUDIENCE as he exits.)*

SIR HENRY. But how did the poor animal know it should run after me?

WATSON *(to AUDIENCE)*. I bet you know if you've been watching closely!

HOLMES. The pair of boots you lost, Sir Henry? Stapleton stole them from your hotel room in London. He had to have something with your scent on it. He brought the boots out to the hound in the barn after he excused himself after dinner.

SIR HENRY. Just as he used my scarf to bring down poor Selden.

DR. MORTIMER. A fascinating account, Miss Holmes. Your uncle would be most proud.

HOLMES. And Dr. Watson, as well, eh? Couldn't have done it without you, Jennie.

WATSON. Thank you, Shirley. Now, why don't you like my perfume?

SIR HENRY. What shall be done about the Stapletons?

LESTRADE. Tie them down for the night, I should think. Take them to the police in the morning.

(MISS STAPLETON begins sobbing uncontrollably.)

MISS STAPLETON. Forgive me, Sir Henry. I was afraid John would harm me if I didn't help him. That's why I warned you to leave. John's insane, he—

(For an instant SIR HENRY and LESTRADE lose their focus and STAPLETON breaks free and gets hold of his revolver.)

ADLIBS *(overlapping)*. Look out! He's free. My fault, sorry! I dropped the ball there. Someone, get him.

STAPLETON. You can't catch me! No one can!

(Laughing maniacally, STAPLETON flees…perhaps jumping out one of the windows or out through the theater! Whatever the choice, he is quickly gone! Out into the dark and forbidding night.)

MISS STAPLETON *(overlapping)*. John! Come back!

LESTRADE *(overlapping)*. After him, Shirley?

MRS. BARRYMORE. No, it's not safe! The beast is out there!

BARRYMORE *(beginning to draw the drapes shut)*. Close the doors! The windows!

WATSON. We have to—

HOLMES *(overlapping, looking out the windows)*. Fog's too thick. We'll catch him when—

(SFX: Gunshots and STAPLETON's terrible screams are heard.

Then the loudest, most frightening, reverberating shrieking, screaming, howling sounds made by any beast that has ever walked the earth!

MISS STAPLETON screams "Oh, John" and falls to the floor. EVERYONE freezes in their tracks as the wailing reverberates through Baskerville Hall.)

WATSON *(to AUDIENCE)*. No one moved. That blood-curdling moan! The sound of darkness itself wailing in the night! And in that instant, we knew the truth…the real truth…that The Hound would be back again! And he would be very, very hungry!

(EVERYONE remains frozen while turning their heads to the AUDIENCE.)

EVERYONE. Until next time! Sleep tight!

(MUSIC and The Sound of The Hound up loud, up strong!

EVERYONE howls with The Hound!

Then…BLACKOUT!)

CURTAIN—END OF PLAY

SCENE AND CHARACTER BREAKDOWN

ACT ONE

Prologue
Settings:
  – Performance space
Characters:
  – Watson, Selected Ensemble Members

SCENE 1 – WHERE'S SHERLOCK?
Settings:
  – Day/Interior – Holmes' study
Characters:
  – Watson, Holmes, Dr. Mortimer, Sir Henry

SCENE 2 – THE HUGO AFFAIR
Settings:
  – Day/Interior – Holmes' study
  – Night/Interior – Baskerville Hall
  – Night/Exterior – Murky Moor
Characters:
  – Watson, Holmes, Dr. Mortimer, Sir Henry, Hugo Baskerville, Maiden, Shepherd One, Shepherd Two, Revelers/Henchmen/Wenches – as numerous as desired

SCENE 3 – THE DEATH OF POOR SIR CHARLES
Settings:
  – Day/Interior – Holmes' study
  – Night/Exterior – Garden at Baskerville Hall

Characters:

    – Watson, Holmes, Dr. Mortimer, Sir Henry, Sir Charles, Optional Characters: garden trees—as numerous as desired

SCENE 4 – A THREATENING LETTER UNDER THE DOOR

Settings:

    – Day/Interior – Holmes' study

Characters:

    – Watson, Holmes, Dr. Mortimer, Sir Henry, Word actors, Selected Ensemble Members: "Five Million Bucks!"

SCENE 5 – THE NIGHT RIDE TO BASKERVILLE HALL

Settings:

    – Night/Interior – Railway passenger car

    – Night/Exterior – Horse carriage on the Murky Moor

    – Night/Exterior – Baskerville Hall

    – Night/Interior – Baskerville Hall

Characters:

    – Watson, Dr. Mortimer, Sir Henry, Perkins, Barrymore, Mrs. Barrymore

SCENE 6 – THE MORNING AFTER THE NIGHT BEFORE

Settings:

    – Day/Interior – Baskerville Hall

Characters:

    – Watson, Sir Henry, Barrymore, Mrs. Barrymore

SCENE 7 – THE MURKY MOOR UP CLOSE AND PERSONAL
Settings:
– Day/Exterior – Murky Moor
Characters:
– Watson, Stapleton, Miss Stapleton, Selected Ensemble Members: "Lepidoptera"

SCENE 8 – FOOTSTEPS DOWN THE HALL
Settings:
– Night/Interior – Baskerville Hall
Characters:
– Watson, Barrymore, Holmes

ACT TWO

Prologue
Settings:
– Performance space
Characters:
– Watson, Holmes, Sir Henry, Dr. Mortimer, Hugo, Maiden, Hugo's Entourage, Sir Charles, Barrymore, Mrs. Barrymore, Stapleton, Miss Stapleton, Selected Ensemble Members

SCENE 1 – THAT GOOFY LOVE STUFF
Settings:
– Day/Exterior – Murky Moor
Characters:
– Watson, Holmes, Sir Henry, Stapleton, Miss Stapleton

SCENE 2 – BARRYMORE DOES THAT CANDLE THING AGAIN

Settings:

– Night/Exterior – Baskerville Hall

– Day/Interior – Holmes' study

Characters:

– Watson, Sir Henry, Holmes, Barrymore, Mrs. Barrymore

SCENE 3 – LAURA SPILLS THE BEANS...ALMOST

Settings:

– Day/Interior – Laura Lyons' parlor

Characters:

– Barrymore, Mrs. Barrymore, Maid, Laura Lyons, Sir Charles, Stapleton

SCENE 4 – DEATH ON THE MOOR

Settings:

– Night/Interior – Baskerville Hall

– Night/Exterior – Murky Moor

Characters:

– Watson, Holmes, Selden, Stapleton, Dr. Mortimer

SCENE 5 – BAITING THE TRAP

Settings:

– Night/Interior – Baskerville Hall

Characters:

– Holmes, Watson, Dr. Mortimer, Selden, Sir Henry, Barrymore, Mrs. Barrymore

SCENE 6 – THE HOUND AT LAST!

Settings:

   – Night/Exterior – Outside Stapletons' dining room

   – Night/Exterior – Murky Moor

Characters:

   – Holmes, Watson, Sir Henry, Stapleton, Lestrade, Dr. Mortimer, Barrymore, The Hound

SCENE 7 – SHIRLEY WRAPS IT ALL UP FOR US

Settings:

   – Night/Interior – Baskerville Hall

Characters:

   – Holmes, Watson, Sir Henry, Stapleton, Lestrade, Dr. Mortimer, Barrymore, Laura Lyons, Miss Stapleton, Sir Charles, Selected Ensemble Members

PRODUCTION NOTES

Staging Options

Consider opening up your entire playing space. Show the back walls, any wing spaces you may have, everything! Then utilize the entire space. People coming and going from multiple directions, wagons or set pieces waiting in the shadows of the wings, and so on. In short, instead of attempting a "real" environment, play up the theatricality of the piece. This choice may require considerable tech support, of course, but would also enlist the contributions of many participants.

Backdrops and Slides

It may be possible to paint a series of backdrops and/or dioramas for the play that can be flown in or brought onto the stage by actors who then unfurl the canvas appropriately. The drops might reveal the bookcases in Holmes' study, the façades of traditional London business shops, the imposing visage of Baskerville Hall, the craggy hills on the Murky Moor, the distant moon, clouds and the like. Slide projections would be equally effective, highlighting the buildings and terrain of the play.

Signs

To quickly establish the setting, mood and locale, consider using placards or signs that can quickly be placed on and removed from standing tripods at either corner of the stage. Or they might be flown in...or even carried across the stage by an actor.

Some signs, as indicated in the script, might identify the location, such as "221B Baker Street" or "Baskerville Hall," while other signs could be more tongue-in-cheek, such as "Dark & Gloomy Moor—7 km," "Baskerville Manor—Next Right," or "Beware Large Drooling Beast." Let your imagination be your guide.

Family Portraits

Since John Stapleton is revealed to be a Baskerville, we should be able to see a slight resemblance between the actor playing Stapleton and the portrait of Sir Hugo Baskerville. A strong likeness is not necessary, of course, and the portrait would be dark and a bit grimy anyway after enduring years of discoloration due to candle smoke.

Baskerville Hall – Using a "dollhouse" Model

As personnel and resources allow, it might be fun to see a large "dollhouse" model of Baskerville Hall placed rather high on a platform. This could be three to five feet high and a similar width. It might even be placed on a turntable. The front steps could be favored in anticipation of Sir Henry's arrival. It could then be turned around to give the audience a sense of the back garden with access to the moor.

Small lights might be placed inside the doll house that could illuminate the path Barrymore takes through the hallways on his way to signaling Selden on the moor. Small lighting instruments, flashing on and off, along with appropriate sound effects, could underscore the threatening atmosphere that permeates the moor.

Fog and Mist

While fog machines can be very effective, they also can be a bit costly. Consider taking a page from Asian symbolist staging techniques that enlist actors to move strips of colored cloth in such a manner so as to suggest the movement of rivers or streams. For this production, strips or rolling mounds of white and gray-toned gauze, moved imaginatively by actors and/or crew members, would create an impressive, ever changing, and ominous ground fog.

Additional Embellishments

To underscore the overall look and feel of the production, consider placing a few costume mannequins in the lobby, creating posters and programs using period typeset and design embellishments, playing popular music of the period, displaying copies of books written by Sir Arthur Conan Doyle, providing tidbits about English manor life and the superstitious beliefs of the period—anything that might enhance the sense of participation in the Baskerville Experience.

Act One – Scene 3 – The Death of Poor Sir Charles

The comic business involving stumbling over and/or stepping on Sir Charles as he lies dead in Baskerville garden is derived from the classic slapstick tradition of commedia farce. Considerable rehearsal is essential to the success of these comic "bits." If rehearsal time is too short to guarantee the precise execution of the slapstick required, everyone—except Watson—can safely step over Sir Charles instead of making contact with his body. They should be looking elsewhere as they are stepping over Sir Charles so the audience will continue to anticipate that someone will actually step on the body. As well, there are no reasons to mutter any apologies.

Only Watson needs to actually trip over or step on the body directly, and she should do so on her final exit from the garden. Consequently, Sir Charles has no reason to be alive again until Watson makes actual contact with his body. When she does so, Sir Charles should come back to life, shake his fist at Watson, say his line, and then melodramatically slump back into his original "dead" position...with one eye open and cocked at the thundering herd gathered in Holmes' study! Watson's exit line remains intact.

Act One – Scene 4 – What Are Those Words I See?

The newspaper in question is *The Times*, of course, but many Americans think of it—and speak of it—as *The London Times* in order to distinguish it from *The New York Times*. Use your best judgment. Also, the type used was called Times Old Roman. It is difficult to find a visual example of Times Old Roman, but Times Ten Roman will suffice. Examples of Times Ten Roman are plentiful. Fonts.com is a dependable source.

DIRECTOR'S NOTES

DIRECTOR'S NOTES

DIRECTOR'S NOTES

DIRECTOR'S NOTES

DIRECTOR'S NOTES